WOMEN'S EMANCIPATION DURING THE PROPHET'S LIFETIME

T0010262

THE MUSLIM FAMILY **AND THE WOMAN'S POSITION**

Volume 7

Abd al-Halim Abu Shuqqah

Translated and Edited by
Adil Salahi

KUBE
PUBLISHING

The Muslim Family and the Woman's Position, Volume 7

First published in England by
Kube Publishing Ltd
Markfield Conference Centre,
Ratby Lane, Markfield,
Leicestershire, LE67 9SY,
United Kingdom
Tel: +44 (0) 1530 249230
Email: info@ kubepublishing.com
Website: www.kubepublishing.com

WOMEN'S EMANCIPATION DURING THE PROPHET'S LIFETIME

Copyright © Adil Salahi 2023
All rights reserved.

The right of Abd al-Halim Abu Shuqqah to be identified as
the author of this work has been asserted by him in accordance
with the Copyright, Designs and Patents Act, 1988.

CIP data for this book is available from the British Library.

ISBN: 978-1-84774-205-6 *Paperback*
ISBN: 978-1-84774-206-3 *Ebook*

Translate and Edit by: Adil Salahi
Cover Design by: Nasir Cadir
Typeset by: nqaddoura@hotmail.com
Printed by: Elma Printing, Turkey

Contents

Transliteration Table v

CHAPTER I: The Islamic View of Marriage 1

CHAPTER II: Proposal and Engagement

Different ways of making a marriage proposal
Seeing the woman 8
The importance of the engagement period 11
Manners to observe 12
The condition of compatibility 13
Is love permissible before the engagement? 14

CHAPTER III: The Dowry 16

CHAPTER IV: The Marriage Contract 21

The Marriage Contract 22
Essentials to be observed in the marriage contract 23

CHAPTER V: The Couple's Equal Rights 29

One: The Right of Care 30
Care: The Basic Comprehensive Right 33

CHAPTER VI: The Couple's Equal Rights 39

Two: Complimentary Rights 40

Marriage Termination 51

The man's right of divorce 51

The woman's right of termination by *khul'* is the same as the man's right of divorce 65

CHAPTER VII: Dealing with Marital Disagreements 68

CHAPTER VIII: More than One Wife 79

Transliteration Table

Consonants. Arabic

initial, unexpressed, medial and final: ء ʾ

ا	a	د	d	ض	ḍ	ك	k
ب	b	ذ	dh	ط	ṭ	ل	l
ت	t	ر	r	ظ	ẓ	م	m
ث	th	ز	z	ع	ʿ	ن	n
ج	j	س	s	غ	gh	هـ	h
ح	ḥ	ش	sh	ف	f	و	w
خ	kh	ص	ṣ	ق	q	ي	y

Vowels, diphthongs, etc.

short:	ـَ	a	ـِ	i	ـُ	u
long:	ـَا	ā	ـُو	ū	ـِي	ī
diphthongs:			ـَوْ	aw		
			ـَيْ	ay		

CHAPTER I

The Islamic View of Marriage

God has made man a source of support for the woman and made the woman a source of peace for man, which makes them incline towards each other. He says: 'Among His signs is that He creates for you spouses out of your own kind, so that you might incline towards them, and He engenders love and tenderness between you. In this there are clear signs indeed for people who think.' (30: 21) When support and inclination are coupled with mutual love and tenderness, then all goodness is available to both man and woman.

The best of life's enjoyment

'Abdullāh ibn 'Amr quotes the Prophet as saying: "The life of this world is but a source of enjoyment, and the best source of enjoyment in this life is a good woman." [Related by Muslim] While a good woman is man's best source of happiness and enjoyment, a good man is likewise the best source of happiness and enjoyment for a woman.

One half of religion

Anas narrated that the Prophet (peace be upon him) said: 'When a person gets married, he completes one half of his religion. He should be God-fearing in how he deals with the other half.' Another version related by al-Ṭabarānī says: 'Whoever gets married completes half of faith. He should be God-fearing in how to deal with the other half.' [Related by al-Bayhaqī in *Shu'ab al-Īmān*] Needless to say, the Prophet's address is to both man and woman.

A believer wife helps in what relates to the future life

Thawbān said that God's Messenger (peace be upon him) said: 'Let everyone of you have a thankful heart, a tongue that glorifies God and a wife who is a believer helping him in what concerns the life to come.' [Related by Ahmad] The same applies to women. A woman should choose a husband who is a believer who helps her in what concerns her future life.

A good woman is a source of happiness

Sa'd said that the Prophet (peace be upon him) said: 'Four things contribute to a person's happiness: a good wife, a spacious home, a good neighbour and a comfortable means of transport.' [Related by al-Ḥākim] Likewise, a woman's happiness is enhanced by a good husband and a good neighbour.

Marriage is the practice of all prophets as well as Prophet Muhammad

God says in the Qur'an: 'We have indeed sent messengers before you and given them wives and offspring.' (13: 38)

Anas ibn Mālik narrated: 'Three men came to the Prophet's homes enquiring from his wives about his worship at home. When they were told the details, they appeared to think that it was less than what is adequate. They said to each other: "Our position is far below that of the Prophet. He has been forgiven all his sins, past, present and future." One of them said: "I will pray all night every night for the rest of my life." The second said: "I will fast every day without fail." The third said: "As for me, I will never marry." The Prophet went to them and said: "Are you the ones who said so and so? By God, I am the most God-fearing person among you, yet I fast some days and do not fast on others, and I pray at night but I also sleep, and I do marry. Such is my tradition and anyone who does not follow my tradition does not belong to me."' [Related by al-Bukhari and Muslim]

The Prophet encourages marriage and rejects celibacy

'Abdullāh ibn Mas'ūd narrated: 'We were young men with the Prophet and had nothing. God's Messenger said to us: "Young men, whoever of you can afford it, should get married. It helps to lower one's gaze and maintain chastity. Whoever cannot afford it should resort to fasting, as it reduces desire.' [Related by al-Bukhari and Muslim]

Sa'd ibn Abi Waqqāṣ reports: 'God's Messenger (peace be upon him) rejected 'Uthmān ibn Maẓ'ūn's wish to remain celibate. Had he permitted him, we would have emasculated ourselves.' [Related by al-Bukhari and Muslim]

The Prophet encourages early marriage for young men and women

'Abd al-Muṭṭalib ibn Rabī'ah ibn al-Ḥārith said that the Prophet (peace be upon him) said to Maḥmiyyah: 'Give your daughter to this young man [al-Faḍl ibn 'Abbās] in marriage', and he did. He also said to Nawfal ibn al-Ḥārith: 'Give this young man [your daughter] as a wife, and he did.' [Related by Muslim]

'Ā'ishah narrated that God's Messenger said: 'Had Usāmah been a girl, I would have given him a good attire and adornment to make him attractive.' Another version of this hadith is: 'By God, had Usāmah been a girl, I would have given her refinements and adornments to make her attractive.' [Related by Ahmad]

The Muslim state should help matrimony

'Abd al-Muṭṭalib ibn Rabī'ah ibn al-Ḥārith said that the Prophet (peace be upon him) said to Maḥmiyyah: 'Takke such-and-such from the one-fifth share and pay it as dowry on their behalf.' [Related by Muslim] This means that the Prophet instructed Maḥmiyyah who was in charge of the share of the Muslim state of war gains [which is one-fifth] to pay the dowry of al-Faḍl ibn 'Abbās and 'Abd al-Muṭṭalib ibn Rabī'ah. This means that the Muslim state may encourage marriage by paying the dowry on behalf of poor Muslims from state funds.

Al-Mustawrid ibn Shaddād said: 'I heard the Prophet (peace be upon him) say: "Whoever is undertaking an assignment for us [i.e. for the Muslim state] should have a wife. If he has no servant, he should have a servant, and if he has no home, he should have a home."' [Related by Abu Dāwūd]

Islam permits giving a woman in her waiting period a hint of a prospective proposal

God says: 'You will incur no sin if you give a hint of a marriage offer to [widowed] women or keep such an intention to yourselves.' (2: 235)

Fāṭimah bint Qays narrated: 'My husband sent me word that he had divorced me... I went to God's Messenger (peace be upon him) and he asked me: "How many times has he divorced you?" I said: "Three times"... He said: "When you have finished your waiting period, let me know."' [Related by Muslim] Thus, the Prophet gave her a hint that she should not get married before telling him. When she finished her waiting period, the Prophet advised her to marry Usāmah ibn Zayd and she did.

Islam facilitates marriage shortly after the end of a woman's waiting period

Al-Miswar ibn Makhramah narrated that 'Subay'ah al-Aslamiyyah gave birth a few days after her husband had died. She came to the Prophet and asked permission to get married. He gave her permission and she got married.' Another version mentions: 'When she finished her postnatal period, she adorned herself for prospective proposals.' [Related by al-Bukhari and Muslim]

Facilitating the marriage procedure including a dowry, contract and publicity

'Uqbah ibn 'Āmir said that God's Messenger (peace be upon him) said: 'The best dowry is what is easiest to give.' [Related by al-Ḥākim]

The marriage contract requires the presence of the woman's guardian. It is also recommended that it is attended by some of the bridegroom's relatives. The minimum attendance required is for two witnesses to be present. 'Ā'ishah said that the Prophet said: 'No marriage is valid unless attended by [the woman's] guardian and two men of integrity as witnesses.' [Related by al-Bayhaqī]

It is also recommended that some aspects of celebration, such as singing and music, should be part of the publicity. Muhammad ibn Ḥāṭib narrated that God's Messenger (peace be upon him) said: 'What distinguishes the lawful from the forbidden in respect of marriage is the tambourine and the singing.' [Related by Ibn Mājah]

‘Abd al-Raḥmān ibn ‘Awf said that when he got married, ‘the Prophet said to me: give a dinner, even if it is only one sheep.’ [Related by al-Bukhari and Muslim]

Such is the religion of Islam. It is keen to make all matters related to marriage easy for all parties. ‘Ā’ishah said that God’s Messenger (peace be upon him) said: ‘An aspect of the blessing of a woman is her easy engagement and easy dowry.’ [Related by Ahmad] ‘Uqbah ibn ‘Āmir narrated that God’s Messenger (peace be upon him) said: ‘The best marriage is the easiest.’ [Related by Abu Dāwūd]

Such is what Islam prescribes for men and women with regard to marriage. A woman attains a great status when she is united with a good and devout man. She brings sunshine into his life. She is like a gentle bird, a rose with a fine scent and a source of happiness.

CHAPTER II

Proposal and Engagement

CHAPTER SUMMARY:

- Different ways of making a marriage proposal
- Seeing the woman
- The importance of the engagement period
- Manners to observe
- The condition of compatibility
- Is love permissible before the engagement?

Proposal and Engagement

Different ways of making a marriage proposal

1. **Approach through the woman's family:** 'Urwah narrated that the Prophet made his proposal to marry 'Ā'ishah to Abu Bakr, [her father]. Abu Bakr said to him: 'But I am your brother.' The Prophet said: 'You are my brother in God's faith and Book, but she is lawful for me to marry.' [Related by al-Bukhari]

   'Umar said: 'The Prophet proposed to me that he marry Ḥafṣah, and I gave her to him in marriage.' [Related by al-Bukhari]
2. **Direct approach to the woman herself: Anas reported:** 'Abu Ṭalḥah made his proposal to Umm Sulaym. She said: "A man like you would never be rejected, but you are an unbeliever and I am a Muslim woman. It is not permissible for me to marry you. If you accept Islam, that will be my dowry, and I will ask you for nothing else." Abu Ṭalḥah embraced Islam and that was her dowry.' [Related by al-Nasā'ī]
3. **The woman's father, or a relative, suggests the marriage to a man of good faith and fine morality:** Al-Bukhari includes a chapter heading: 'A man offers his daughter as a wife to a good

person.' This reminds us of what God mentions in the Qur'an of the Madyan old man when he offered one of his two daughters as a wife to Moses (peace be upon him). God says: '[The father] said: "I will give you one of these two daughters of mine in marriage on the understanding that you will remain eight years in my service. If you should complete ten years, it will be of your own choice. I do not wish to impose any hardship on you. You will find me, if God so wills, an upright man.' Answered [Moses]: 'This is agreed between me and you. Whichever of the two terms I fulfil, I trust I shall not be wronged. God is the witness to all we say.' (28: 27-8)

4. **The man puts his proposal through the chief of the community, or the chief makes a proposal on behalf of someone else:** 'Uqbah ibn 'Āmir narrated that the Prophet said to one man: 'Do you agree to marry this woman?' He said: 'Yes.' The Prophet asked the woman: 'Do you agree to marry this man?' She said: 'Yes.' The Prophet married them and the marriage was then consummated. [Related by Abu Dāwūd]
5. **A woman offers marriage to a good person:** Thābit al-Bunānī narrated: 'I was visiting Anas and one of his daughters was present. Anas said: "A woman came to the Prophet (peace be upon him) offering herself [as a wife] to him. She said: 'Messenger of God, will you accept me?' [In another version, she said: Messenger of God, I have come to offer myself as a present to you] Anas's daughter said: "How impolite! What a shame! What a shame!" Anas said: "She is better than you. She wished to marry the Prophet and she offered herself to him."' [Related by al-Bukhari]
6. **Giving a hint of intended proposal during the waiting period [of a widow or a finally-divorced woman]:** God says: 'You will incur no sin if you give a hint of a marriage offer to [widowed] women or keep such an intention to yourselves. God knows that you will entertain such intentions concerning them. Do not, however, plight your troth in secret; but speak only in a decent manner. Furthermore, do not resolve on actually making the marriage tie before the prescribed term [of waiting] has run its course. Know

well that God knows what is in your minds, so have fear of Him; and know that God is much-forgiving, clement.' (2: 235)

Seeing the woman

Sahl ibn Sā'idah narrated: 'A woman came to the Prophet and said: "Messenger of God! I have come to make of myself a present to you." The Prophet looked her up and down several times, then he lowered his head.' [Related by al-Bukhari and Muslim]

Al-Mughīrah ibn Shu'bah said that he proposed marriage to a woman. The Prophet said to him: 'Look at her. This should enhance good feelings between the two of you.' [Related by al-Tirmidhī]

Muhammad ibn Maslamah said: 'I proposed to a woman. I then resorted to hiding until I saw her when she was on a palm date farm.' People said to him: 'Do you do that when you are a Companion of the Prophet?' He said: I heard God's Messenger (peace be upon him) say: "If God puts in a man's heart the intention to propose to a woman, it is permissible for him to look at her."' [Related by Ibn Mājah]

Ibn Ja'far said that 'Umar ibn al-Khaṭṭāb proposed to marry 'Alī's daughter, but he mentioned that she was young. People said to him: He has refused you; so ask him again. ['Alī] said: 'I will send her to you to look at.' He was satisfied with her, and he uncovered her shins. She said: 'Hold back. Were you not *Amīr al-Mu'minīn*, I would have given you a black eye.' [Mentioned in Ibn Qudāmah's *al-Mughnī*]

We draw readers' attention to the fact that there is no harm if a woman applies her visible makeup so that she may receive a marriage proposal. In fact, Islam goes beyond merely allowing this.

1. *Al-Mughnī*, Vol. 7, p. 18. This is one of the most important books of the Ḥanbalī School of Fiqh.

It prefers that a Muslim woman should have such apparent makeup generally. This is even more desirable if she is hoping for a marriage proposal. We mentioned in Chapter 1 the hadith that says: 'By God, had Usāmah been a girl, I would have given her refinements and adornments to make her attractive.' [Related by Ahmad]

The importance of the engagement period

The first step is that the man looks at the woman without her knowledge, in order to spare her any disappointment, if he decides not to proceed. The second step is when the man decides to put his proposal to the woman's family. Her family must put the matter to her to decide. They need to make it easy for the man and woman to see each other and get to know each other and their respective personalities. God's Messenger (peace be upon him) said: 'One feature of the goodness of a woman is to facilitate her engagement.' [Related by Ahmad]

Seeking God's guidance, i.e. *istikhārah*: When both the man and the woman feel happy to proceed with the engagement, it is desirable for each of them to seek God's guidance and pray to Him to facilitate it. Jābir ibn 'Abdullāh reports: 'The Prophet (peace be upon him) used to teach us the *istikhārah* (i.e. seeking guidance) in all matters just as he would teach us a surah of the Qur'an: "When a person is about to decide something, let him pray two *rak'ahs* then say: 'My Lord, I seek the help of Your knowledge in making a choice and seek Your assistance based on Your power and appeal to You to bestow on me some of Your limitless favour, for You are powerful and I am not and You know all while I do not. You are the One who knows all that cannot be perceived. My Lord, if You know this matter [the supplicant should specify the matter] is beneficial to me in my faith, my livelihood and in the outcome of my affairs - (or he said: in my short-term and long-term affairs) - then grant it to me, facilitate and bless it for me. But if You know this matter [the supplicant should specify it again] is disadvantageous for me in my faith, my livelihood, and in the outcome of my affairs - (or he said: in my short-term and long-term affairs) - then keep it away from me and keep me away from it. Give me what is good for me whatever it may be and make me happy with it.' He added that one should state the matter he seeks guidance on. [Related by al-Bukhari]

Two questions are often asked about looking at the woman one intends to propose to. The first question asks whether the woman should see the man, because the hadith does not mention this. In answer, we say that the Prophet told al-Mughīrah: 'Look at her. This should enhance good feelings between the two of you.' This purpose is better served if the woman also sees the one proposing to marry her and she is satisfied with him. The other question wonders whether the two parties should have a meeting to exchange views and get to know each other. In answer, we cite the Prophet's hadith: 'If he can look at what encourages him to marry her, he should do so.'

Manners to observe

- No counter proposal: Nāfi' reported that Ibn 'Umar used to say: 'God's Messenger (peace be upon him) prohibited a person from trying to undersell his brother, or that a man makes a proposal of marriage to a woman when his brother has already proposed to her, until the first suitor has abandoned the matter or given him permission.' [Related by al-Bukhari and Muslim]
- A suitor is a stranger: A proposal of marriage is a preliminary step, not a binding contract. Therefore, the man who has submitted a marriage proposal is not allowed anything beyond what is permissible to a stranger. The woman proposed to should adhere to the same manners as when she meets strangers: she wears a full attire, covering all her body except her face and hands, and she may not be in seclusion with her suitor.

- Encouragement of meeting and gifts: Meetings of the suitor and his intended, in the presence of some of her immediate relatives, should enable the two parties to get to know each other, particularly in our modern societies. As for giving gifts, the Prophet said: 'Exchange gifts to promote love and amity.' When a suitor gives a gift to his intended, he hopes to ensure harmony between them.

The condition of compatibility

Abu Hurayrah narrated that the Prophet (peace be upon him) said: 'A woman is sought in marriage for any of four qualities: her wealth, lineage, beauty and religion. Make sure to choose the one who is religious.' [Related by al-Bukhari and Muslim]

Sahl ibn Sa'd reports: 'A man passed by God's Messenger (peace be upon him) and the Prophet said to someone sitting with him: "What do you think of this man?" The man said: "This is one of the elite. If he comes with a marriage proposal, he is likely to be accepted, and if he intercedes, his intercession is likely to be granted." The Prophet did not say anything. Another man passed by and the Prophet said to the same man: "What do you think of this man?" The man replied: "Messenger of God, this is one of the poor among Muslims. He is unlikely to be accepted if he comes with a marriage proposal; if he intercedes, his intercession is unlikely to be accepted; and if he speaks, he is unlikely to be listened to." The Prophet said: "This one is better than the earth's fill of the first one."' [Related by al-Bukhari]

From this hadith we conclude that Islam gives top priority to compatibility in faith and morality. This is further emphasized by the Prophet as he says: 'Be selective when you choose for your offspring. Marry those who are compatible with you and give your women in marriage to them.' [Related by Ibn Mājah] He also says: 'If a man whose piety and manners you find satisfactory comes to you with a proposal of marriage, then accept his proposal. Unless you do, there will be strife on earth and much corruption.' [Related by al-Tirmidhī]

Is love permissible before the engagement?

From the Qur'an: God says: "You will incur no sin if you give a hint of a marriage offer to [widowed] women or keep such an intention to yourselves. God knows that you will entertain such intentions concerning them. Do not, however, plight your troth in secret; but speak only in a decent manner. Furthermore, do not resolve on actually making the marriage tie before the prescribed term [of waiting] has run its course. Know well that God knows what is in your minds, so have fear of Him; and know that God is much-forgiving, clement."' (2: 235)

This verse gives a general statement that allows all levels of emotion. In his commentary on the Qur'an, al-Ṭabarī quotes several statements of explanation which also allow these levels. These statements include: Al-Suddī said: 'He comes in, says his greetings, gives a gift if he wishes, but says nothing else.' Al-Qāsim ibn Muhammad said that he may say something like: 'I am inclined towards you. I am keen to be with you. I admire you.' Ibn 'Abbās said that he may say: 'I would like a woman whose character is such-and-such.' Mālik said that he may say: 'I admire you and I like you.'

From the Sunnah: The Sunnah encourages the desire to marry any good and devout woman, but it also approves of admiring a particular woman. Anas reports on the Battle of Khaybar. He says: 'We took it over after a hard battle. The captives were assembled. Diḥyah came over and said: "Prophet, give me a maid from the captives." He said: "Go and choose one"... He took Ṣafiyyah bint Ḥuyay. A man came to the Prophet and said: "Prophet of God, you have given Ṣafiyyah bint Ḥuyay, the mistress of Qurayẓah and al-Naḍīr, to Diḥyah. She is suitable for none other than you." The Prophet said: "Call him to bring her." When he brought her, the Prophet looked at her. He said to him: "Choose a different captive." The Prophet set her free and married her.' [Related by al-Bukhari and Muslim]

It is normal that a man should love a particular woman. Ibn ʿAbbās narrated: 'A man came to the Prophet and said: We have an orphan girl, and she has been proposed to by one poor person and another who is rich. She loves the poor one and we prefer the rich one. The Prophet (peace be upon him) said: "Nothing is seen better to a loving couple than marriage."' [Related by Ibn Mājah]

It is also perfectly appropriate for a woman to desire to marry a devout person. Saʿīd ibn Khālid reports that Umm Ḥakīm bint Qāriẓ said to ʿAbd al-Raḥmān ibn ʿAwf: 'More than one person has proposed to me. Marry me to whoever of them you choose.' He said: 'Are you leaving this decision to me?' She said: 'Yes.' He said: 'I will marry you myself.' [Related by Ibn Saʿd]

CHAPTER III

The Dowry

The dowry is obligatory and it rightfully belongs to the woman, with no one else having a claim to it. Marriage is not valid without a dowry. God says in the Qur'an: 'Give women their dowry as a free gift.' (4: 4) An orphan girl must be given her fair dowry, which should be similar to what women of her social status receive. God says: 'If you fear that you may not deal fairly by the orphans, you may marry of other women as may be agreeable to you.' (4: 3)

'Urwah ibn al-Zubayr mentions that he asked 'Ā'ishah about the meaning of the verse which says: 'If you fear that you may not deal fairly by the orphans, you may marry of other women as may be agreeable to you.' (4: 3) She answered: 'Nephew, this refers to an orphan girl being brought up by her guardian. He is attracted by her beauty and wealth but wishes not to pay her a full dowry. This order is given that they must not marry such girls unless they pay them their full dowry.' [Related by al-Bukhari]

The best dowry is that which is easiest to provide. 'Uqbah ibn 'Āmir narrated that God's Messenger (peace be upon him) said: 'The best dowry is the easiest to meet.' [Related by al-Ḥākim] However, there is no minimum or maximum amount of a dowry. It is preferable that the whole amount of the dowry, or a portion of it, is paid before the marriage is consummated. Yet, it is permissible to defer its payment, but whatever of the dowry is deferred remains a debt owed by the husband to his wife.

When a man divorces his wife, he pays her any portion of her agreed dowry he has not already paid her. In addition, he gives her a gift, as stated in the Qur'an: 'Divorced women shall have a provision according to what is fair. This is an obligation on the God-fearing.' (2: 241) If the divorce takes place before the marriage has been consummated, she is entitled to receive a suitable gift if no dowry has been determined. If the amount of the dowry has been agreed, she is entitled to half of it. God says: You will incur no sin if you divorce women before having touched them or settled a dowry for them. Provide for them, the rich according to his means and the straitened according to his means. Such a provision, in an equitable manner, is an obligation binding on the righteous. If you divorce them before having touched them but after having settled a dowry for them, then give them half of that which you have settled, unless they forgo it or he in whose hand is the marriage tie forgoes it. To forgo what is due to you is closer to being righteous. Do not forget to act benevolently to one another. God sees all that you do.' (2: 236–7)

If the husband dies before the marriage is consummated, the dowry remains owed to his widow in full. Likewise, the husband does not claim any portion of the dowry if he divorces his wife after consummation. God says: 'If you wish to take one wife in place of another and you have given the first one a large dowry, do not take away anything of it. Would you take it away though that constitutes a gross injustice and a manifest sin?' (4: 20)

Nor can a husband claim any refund of his dowry if he exchanges mutual curses with his wife. This is the case when a man accuses his wife of adultery and cannot produce any witnesses. They swear five oaths each in confirmation of their claims, i.e. the husband's accusation and the wife's denial. This constitutes a final dissolution of the marriage. Sa'īd ibn Jubayr said: 'I asked Ibn 'Umar about the couple who exchange curses. He told me that the Prophet said to the couple who did this: "You will be accountable to God, as one of you is a liar. [He said to the man]: You have no right to her." The man said: "My money." The Prophet said: "You get nothing. If you had told the truth in your accusation, the dowry is for her being your lawful wife."' [Related by al-Bukhari and Muslim]

The only case in which a man may be given a full or partial refund of the dowry is when his wife resorts to *khul'*, which is the termination of the marriage at the wife's request. God says in the Qur'an: 'Divorce may be [revoked] twice, whereupon a woman may either be retained in fairness or released with kindness. It is unlawful for you to take back from women anything of what you have given them [as dowry], unless they both [husband and wife] fear that they may not be able to keep within the bounds set by God. If you have cause to fear that they would not be able to keep within the bounds set by God, it shall be no offence for either of them if she gives up whatever she may in order to free herself. These are the bounds set by God; do not, then, transgress them. Those who transgress the bounds set by God are wrongdoers indeed.' (2: 229)

God mentions in this verse, 'It shall be no offence for either of them if she gives up whatever she may in order to free herself.' This means that if the woman wants to leave her husband and terminate the marriage, she offers compensation to free herself. This is given out of what her husband might have given her of dowry or other things. There is no harm in the woman offering it, or the man accepting it. Ibn 'Abbās narrated: 'Thābit ibn Qays's wife came to the Prophet and said: "Messenger of God! I do not take anything against Thābit, either with regard to his faith or manners, but I am worried lest I should be ungrateful." The Prophet asked her: "Are you prepared to give him back his garden?" She said: "Yes," and she returned his garden to him. The Prophet ordered him to leave her.' [Related by al-Bukhari]

2. She was unhappy in her marriage because she disliked her husband despite her acknowledgement that he was blameless. She feared that her dislike might lead her to be negligent of her responsibilities as also ungrateful towards him.

CHAPTER IV

The Marriage Contract

- Essentials to be observed in the marriage contract

The Marriage Contract

God says in the Qur'an: 'How can you take it away when each of you has been privy with the other, and they have received from you a most solemn pledge?' (4: 21) In his commentary on the Qur'an, al-Ṭabarī quotes Qatādah explaining this verse: 'The solemn pledge which God has taken for women is either being retained in fairness or released with kindness. It was part of the solemnity at the time of the marriage contract: You owe it before God that you retain her with fairness and release her with kindness.'

In reference to the marriage contract, Ibn al-Qayyim says: 'The purpose of the special mourning when a woman's husband dies is to show the importance and nobility of the marriage contract and that God gives it that. Hence, the waiting period is made as its sanctity, and the mourning as an emphasis of this sanctity. Thus, a wife is required to do this in the case of her husband's death, but not for her father, son, brother or any other relative. This is an aspect of the high status attached to this contract, emphasizing the difference between it and an illegitimate relationship. Therefore, its very beginning is recommended as an announcement, one that is witnessed and celebrated with music, so as to show the contrast between it and an unlawful relationship. At its end, the waiting period and mourning are required, while they are not required in any other situation.'

Essentials to be observed in the marriage contract

1. The woman's right of choice of her husband. Abu Hurayrah said that the Prophet said: 'A previously married woman may not be married again unless she is consulted, and a virgin may not be married without her consent.' [Related by al-Bukhari and Muslim] 'Ā'ishah said: 'Messenger of God, an unmarried woman feels shy. He said: "Her silence shows her consent."' [Related by al-Bukhari]
2. The woman's guardian's agreement is essential. Abu Mūsā reported that the Prophet said: 'No marriage may be done without the presence of the woman's guardian.' [Related by Abu Dāwūd]
3. The presence of the woman's guardian when the marriage contract is done. 'Ā'ishah narrated that God's Messenger (peace be upon him) said: 'No marriage may be done without the presence of the woman's guardian. The ruler is the guardian of anyone who has no guardian.' [Related by Ahmad] 'Imrān said: 'God's Messenger (peace be upon him) said: "No marriage may be done without the presence of the woman's guardian and two persons of integrity as witnesses."' [Related by al-Bayhaqī]

   Imam Ibn Ḥajar said: 'Scholars hold different views concerning the condition of the presence of the woman's guardian at the time when the marriage contract is done. The majority of scholars agree that his presence is essential. They said: "In the first place, a woman may not act on her own behalf in the marriage contract."'
4. Conditions stipulated in the marriage contract must be fulfilled. 'Uqbah narrated that the Prophet (peace be upon him) said: 'The conditions that have the top claim for fulfilment are those that make your wives lawful for you.' [Related by al-Bukhari and Muslim]

However, there are some conditions that are not permissible to stipulate. Abu Hurayrah quotes the Prophet (peace be upon him): 'It is not permissible for a woman to request the divorce of her sister so as to have it all for herself. She may have only the share granted to her.' [Related by al-Bukhari] This applies to a woman who agrees to marry an already married man, but she asks him to divorce his other wife, so that she will be his only wife. This is not permissible, as the hadith states.

5. Publicizing the marriage:

   - Publicity is a duty. Habbār ibn al-Aswad narrated that the Prophet (peace be upon him) said: 'Proclaim the marriage and publicize it.' [Related by al-Ṭabarānī] Abu Mūsā said: The Prophet (peace be upon him) said: "No marriage may be done without the presence of the woman's guardian and two witnesses." [Related by al-Ṭabarānī] The presence of two witnesses is the minimum publicity required, but it is not the recommended practice. What is recommended is that the relatives, neighbours and friends of both spouses be informed of the marriage and that this should be coupled with a celebration.
   - Entertainment. 'Ā'ishah mentions that she attended a woman's wedding to an Anṣārī man. The Prophet said: "'Ā'ishah, was there no entertainment with you? The Anṣār like to have some entertainment.' [Related by al-Bukhari] Imam ibn Ḥajar commented on the Prophet's question, 'was there no entertainment with you?' He points out that in Sharīk's narration of the hadith, which is related by al-Ṭabarānī, the Prophet said: 'Should you have not sent her a maid who plays the tambourine and sings?' I said: 'What would she sing?' The Prophet answered: 'She would say:

     We have come to you; we have come to you. Greetings
     to us, and greetings to you.

Had it not been for the red gold, she would not have come near your quarters.
And had it not been for the dark wheat, your girls would not have been plump.'

Habbār ibn al-Aswad mentions that he gave his daughter away in marriage. They had a large drum and several tambourines. When the Prophet came out, he heard the noise and asked: 'What is it?' People said: 'Habbār's wedding.' The Prophet said: 'Publicize the marriage; publicize the marriage. This is marriage, not an unlawful relationship.' [Related by Ibn Mandah]

- Women's attendance at the wedding, their presentation of the bride to her husband and supplication for blessing. 'Ā'ishah narrated: 'The Prophet married me... My mother, Umm Rūman, came over. She took me inside where there were several women from the Anṣār. They said: "With all goodness and blessings! With all future happiness."' [Related by al-Bukhari and Muslim] Likewise, men pray to God to bless the two spouses. Anas ibn Mālik narrated that the Prophet noticed traces of saffron on 'Abd al-Raḥmān ibn 'Awf. He asked him about it. He said: "I have married an Anṣārī woman giving a dowry of the weight of a date stone in gold." The Prophet said: "May God make it a blessing for you."' [Related by al-Bukhari and Muslim] Abu Hurayrah mentions that when the Prophet supplicated for a man on his marriage, he would say: 'May God make it a blessing for you and a blessing around you. May He unite the two of you in all that is good.' [Related by al-Tirmidhī]
- The wedding dinner. It is strongly recommended that the bridegroom gives a dinner shortly after the marriage, inviting relatives and neighbours. Anas said: 'The Prophet did not give any of his wives a wedding dinner as large as he did for Zaynab. He slaughtered a sheep.' [Related by al-Bukhari and

Muslim] ʿAbd al-Raḥmān ibn ʿAwf said: ʿThe Prophet said to me [when I got married]: "Give a dinner, even if you sacrifice a sheep."' [Related by al-Bukhari and Muslim] Al-Bukhari enters this hadith under the chapter heading: 'A wedding dinner is a duty.'

- Attending the wedding dinner. ʿAbdullāh ibn ʿUmar narrated that God's Messenger (peace be upon him) said: 'Accept this invitation if you are invited.' ʿAbdullāh himself would accept any invitation to a meal, whether for a wedding or any other occasion, even if he was fasting. [Related by al-Bukhari and Muslim]

  ʿAbdullāh ibn ʿUmar narrated that God's Messenger (peace be upon him) said: 'When any of you is invited to a wedding dinner, he should attend.' Another version narrated by Abu Hurayrah quotes the Prophet: 'Whoever declines an invitation disobeys God and His Messenger.' [Related by al-Bukhari and Muslim]

6. Manners to be observed at the consummation of the marriage:

- Starting with prayer and supplication. Ibn ʿAbbās narrated that the Prophet (peace be upon him) said: 'When a person is about to have intercourse with his wife he should say: "My Lord, keep Satan away from me and keep him away from what You give us." If he does and a child is given them as a result, no devil shall ever harm it.' [Related by al-Bukhari]

  Abu Wā'il reports: 'A man from Bujaylah came to ʿAbdullāh [i.e. Ibn Masʿūd] and said: "I have married a virgin girl and I fear that she may dislike me." ʿAbdullāh said: "Good companionship is from God and abhorrence is from Satan, as he makes them loathe each other. When you are privy with her, let her stand behind you and [the two of you] offer a prayer of two *rakʿahs*." Then supplicate: "My Lord, grant me a blessing with my family and grant my family a blessing with me. Give them from me and give me from them. My Lord, as long as you keep us together, unite us for all that is good, and if You part us, let our parting be to what is good."' [Related by al-Ṭabarānī]

- Some entertainment in the morning after the wedding. Khālid ibn Dhakwān narrated from al-Rubayyiʿ bint Muʿawwidh ibn ʿAfrā.' She said: 'The Prophet (peace be upon him) visited me in the morning after my wedding. He sat on my bed, in the same position as you are seated now. Some of our maids played the tambourine and sang the praises of my fathers [i.e. father and uncles] killed in the Battle of Badr. One of them said: "Among us is a Prophet who knows what will happen tomorrow." The Prophet said to her: "Forget this and go back to what you were saying earlier."' [Related by al-Bukhari]
- Gifts to the bride and bridegroom. Anas ibn Mālik narrated: 'After the Prophet's wedding to Zaynab, Umm Sulaym said to me: "I think we should send God's Messenger a gift." I said: "Do that." She put together some dates, butter and dried milk and cooked a dish in a saucepan. She gave me the saucepan to take to him. I carried it to him. He said to me: "Put it down." He then said: "Invite for me these people, naming them, and invite everyone you meet."' [Related by al-Bukhari and Muslim]

CHAPTER V

The Couple's Equal Rights

- One: The Right of Care
- Care: The Basic Comprehensive Right

One: The Right of Care

God says: 'Women shall, in all fairness, enjoy rights similar to those exercised against them, although men have an advantage over them. God is almighty, wise.' (2: 228) This Qur'anic verse confirms that women have rights equal to the duties they have to fulfil. This means that every right the woman has is mirrored by a right belonging to the man. Therefore, their rights are equal. Ibn 'Abbās said: 'I like to attend to my appearance for my wife just as I love that she adorns herself for me, because God, the Exalted, says: 'Women shall, in all fairness, enjoy rights similar to those exercised against them.'

Al-Ṭabarī mentions several reports explaining the meaning of the next clause in the verse, 'although men have an advantage over them.' He said that this advantage refers to whatever he gifts her, performing whatever duty he owes to her and overlooking all or part of her duty towards him. Ibn 'Abbās said: 'I do not like to take all the right she owes to me, because God, the Exalted, says: 'although men have an advantage over them.'

Muhammad Mahmood Shakir, the scholar who edited al-Ṭabarī's commentary on the Qur'an, wrote:

> Abu Ja'far [al-Ṭabarī] did not write this to give men some admonition... He provided the proof and binding evidence, deducing this from the Qur'anic verses as they are recited in succession... The sequence of verses shows that the man's rights against the woman are equal to her rights against him. He follows this by encouraging men to attain a merit which can only be attained by resolve and nobility. This is to forgo some of the man's rights which his wife owes to him. If he does this, then he attains a degree of fine manners that gives him an advantage over his wife. Acting on this fine understanding of the meanings of the Qur'an, a Book of superior literary excellence, Abu Ja'far suggests a different sense of this sentence, 'although men have an advantage over them.' He shows that it urges men to try to attain a superior grade. To him, the sentence does not speak of a favour God has given to men, whether they do His bidding well or poorly.

Similar recommendations

In His infinite wisdom, God follows the establishment of equal rights with similar recommendations for both husband and wife, so that tenderness and love prevail in their family life, and each of them takes good and perfect care of the other.

Recommendations addressed to men include the Qur'anic verse: 'Consort with them in a goodly manner. Even if you are averse to them, it may well be that you are averse to something in which God has placed much good.' (4: 19) Abu Hurayrah said that the Prophet (peace be upon him) said: 'Take good care of women.' [Related by al-Bukhari and Muslim] Ibn 'Abbās narrated from the Prophet (peace be upon him): 'The best of you are those who are best to their wives, and I am the best of you to my wives.' [Related by Ibn Mājah] 'Abdullāh ibn 'Amr ibn al-'Āṣ said that the Prophet said: 'The best of you are those who are best to their women.' [Related by Ibn Mājah]

Recommendations addressed to women include: Abu Hurayrah quotes the Prophet as saying: 'The best women to ride camels are the good ones among the Quraysh women: they are the most caring of children when they are young, and the most considerate of husbands regarding their money.' [Related by al-Bukhari and Muslim] Abu Udhaynah narrated that the Prophet (peace be upon him) said: 'The best of your women is the motherly, friendly, caring and obedient.' [Related by al-Bayhaqī] 'Abdullāh ibn Sallām said that the Prophet (peace be upon him) said: 'The best of women is the one who pleases you when you look at her, obeys you when you require something of her and guards your honour, in respect of herself and your property, during your absence.' [Related by al-Ṭabarānī] 'Abdullāh ibn Abi Awfā narrated from the Prophet (peace be upon him): 'A woman does not fulfil her duties towards God unless she fulfils her duties towards her husband.' [Related by Ibn Mājah] Anas said that God's Messenger (peace be upon him) said: 'When a woman has prayed her five obligatory prayers, fasted her month [of Ramadan], maintained her chastity and obeyed her husband, she ensures her entry into Heaven.' [Related by al-Bazzār]

The general framework of the fulfilment of rights and duties: God says: 'And among His signs is that He creates for you spouses out of your own kind, so that you might incline towards them, and He engenders love and tenderness between you. In this there are clear signs indeed for people who think.' (30: 21)

There are identical rights owed to both husband and wife, such as care, gentle treatment, compassion, having children, mutual trust, sharing interests and concerns, adornment, sexual fulfilment, relaxation, protection and amicable divorce if it is necessary. We shall now discuss these in some detail.

Care: The Basic Comprehensive Right

In a detailed and comprehensive hadith, the Prophet (peace be upon him) makes clear that care is the basic and most important right. ‘Abdullāh ibn ‘Umar quotes the Prophet as saying: ‘Every one of you is a shepherd and accountable for those under his care. The ruler is a shepherd and he is responsible for his subjects. A man is a shepherd of his household and is accountable for his flock. A woman is a shepherd in her husband’s home and for children; and she is accountable for what is under her care.’ [Related by al-Bukhari and Muslim]

This right of care places two very important types of responsibility on both husband and wife. The man undertakes the responsibility of being the head of the family and the responsibility of paying its expenses. The woman undertakes the responsibilities of looking after the children and managing the household’s affairs.

The husband’s first responsibility: God says: ‘Men shall have full care of women.’ (4: 34) In his commentary on the Qur’an, *al-Jāmi‘ li-Aḥkām al-Qur’an*, al-Qurṭubī mentions that Ibn ‘Abbās explains the Qur'anic statement, 'although men shall have an advantage over them.' He says: 'This urges men to treat women with kindness and to ensure their comfort in money and manners. This means that the husband should exert himself to ensure this.' Ibn 'Aṭiyyah said: 'This is a fine and correct view.'

We may add that the 'headship' in the family is not dictatorial. On the contrary, it is based on consultation, because consultation is an essential part of a Muslim's behaviour in all affairs. Moreover, it is controlled by a full list of religious rules, including the most important one, which is stated in the Qur'an: 'Women shall, in all fairness, enjoy rights similar to those exercised against them.' (2: 228) Further, it is controlled by all the rulings concerning marriage, divorce and mutual treatment, as well as all the moral values that govern human life and guide it to what is best. Most importantly, headship in the family is based on love and tenderness.

Both man and wife should cooperate to ensure progress of the family in the right direction. Such cooperation may have several aspects, such as: (1) The wife's obedience. The Prophet says: 'No one may be obeyed in what constitutes disobedience of God. Obedience only applies in what is lawful.' [Related by Muslim] (2) Consultation between husband and wife regarding all concerns of the family. (3) The wife acting as deputy for her husband when he travels, undertaking the management of all family affairs.

The husband's second responsibility: Paying the life expenses of the family is man's responsibility, and it is based on the fact that he can devote his time to earning income. God says: 'Men shall take full care of women with the bounties with which God has favoured some of them more abundantly than others, and with what they may spend of their own wealth.' (4: 34) Jābir ibn 'Abdullāh narrated that God's Messenger (peace be upon him) said: 'It is your duty towards them that you be responsible to provide in a fair manner for their sustenance and clothing.' [Related by Muslim] Abu Mas'ūd al-Anṣārī quotes the Prophet (peace be upon him): 'When a Muslim willingly spends on his family, and he seeks God's acceptance, what he spends is counted as a charity he gives.' [Related by al-Bukhari and Muslim] Sa'd ibn Abi Waqqāṣ narrated that the Prophet visited him when he was ill in Makkah... [The Prophet] said to him: 'Whatever you spend is counted as a charity you have given, even including a bite you place in your wife's mouth....' [Related by al-Bukhari and Muslim]

Both man and wife can cooperate for the proper fulfilment of paying the expenses of the family. This may be in different ways, such as:

- A wife may spend out of her husband's money on their family, in a reasonable manner. This may be without the husband's knowledge if he is stingy. 'Ā'ishah narrated that 'Hind bint 'Utbah said to the Prophet: 'Messenger of God! Abu Sufyān [her husband] is stingy. He does not give me enough to look after myself and my children, unless I take from him without his knowledge.' He said to her: 'Take what is sufficient for you and your children in a reasonable manner.' [Related by al-Bukhari and Muslim]
- A wife may give in charity out of her husband's money, in a reasonable manner. 'Ā'ishah said that God's Messenger (peace be upon him) said: 'If a woman gives in charity some of the food of her household, without causing shortage, she earns a reward for what she has given, and her husband earns a reward for what he had earned.' [Related by al-Bukhari and Muslim]
- A wife may give a gift out of her husband's money, in a reasonable manner. Anas narrated: 'God's Messenger got married and consummated his marriage. My mother cooked *ḥays* [a dish made of dried milk, dates and butter] and put it in a stone jug. She said: "Anas, take this to God's Messenger and say: my mother has sent this to you with her greetings,

and she says that this is too little from us to you, Messenger of God." I took it to God's Messenger (peace be upon him) and said: My mother has sent this to you with her greetings, and she says that this is too little from us to you, Messenger of God. He said to me: "Put it down." He then said: "Invite for me these people, naming them, and invite everyone you meet."' [Related by al-Bukhari and Muslim. This is Muslim's version]

A wife may help her husband if he is poor. Zaynab, ʿAbdullāh ibn Masʿūd's wife, reports that God's Messenger (peace be upon him) said: "Women, give to charity, even though you may have to give of your jewellery." I went home and said to ʿAbdullāh: "You are a man of limited means, and God's Messenger (peace be upon him) has ordered us to give to charity. Go and ask him if it is acceptable to give it to you. Otherwise, I will pay it to someone else." ʿAbdullāh said: "You go to him." Zaynab said: "I went to the Prophet and I found at his door a woman from the Anṣār having come to ask the same question I wanted to ask... The Prophet said: 'Yes, and they earn a double reward: the reward of giving to relatives and the reward of paying zakat'." [Related by al-Bukhari and Muslim, and this is Muslim's version]

Abu Saʿīd al-Khudrī narrated: 'Zaynab, Ibn Masʿūd's wife came over and said: "Prophet, today you ordered us to pay charity, and I have some jewellery which I wanted to give away. Ibn Masʿūd claims that he and his children are the most entitled to have this charity.' The Prophet said: 'Ibn Masʿūd is right. Your husband and children are the most entitled to have your charity.' [Related by al-Bukhari]

- A wife consults her husband on spending her money. ʿAbdullāh narrated: 'When God's Messenger (peace be upon him) took over Makkah, he addressed the people. He said in his speech: "It is not permissible for a woman to give away without her husband's permission."' [Related by al-Nasā'ī] Wāthilah said that God's Messenger (peace be upon him) said: 'It is not permissible for a woman to spend a large amount of her money without her husband's permission.' While consultation is a commendable action which a Muslim is recommended to do concerning his general affairs, it is more important between husband and wife, so that family ties are strengthened.

The wife's first responsibility is looking after her children: The Qur'an establishes the woman's responsibility for her children and taking care of them. It stresses the hardship she goes through during her pregnancy and childbirth. In fact, her responsibility for her child and taking care of it does not start at childbirth; it starts from the moment she becomes pregnant. God says in the Qur'an: 'We have enjoined upon man to show kindness to his parents: in pain did his mother bear him, and in pain did she give him birth. His bearing and weaning takes thirty months.' (46: 15) 'We have enjoined upon man goodness to his parents: his mother bore him going from weakness to weakness, and his weaning takes place within two years. Be grateful to Me and to your parents. With Me is the end of all journeys.' (31: 14) 'Mothers may breast-feed their children for two whole years; [that is] for those who wish to complete the suckling.' (2: 233)

The Prophet stated the woman's responsibility for looking after her children. 'Abdullāh ibn 'Umar quotes the Prophet as saying: 'Everyone of you is a shepherd and accountable for those under his care... A woman is a shepherd in her husband's home and for their children; and she is accountable for what is under her care.' [Related by al-Bukhari and Muslim] The Prophet also praised the women who take good care of their children. Abu Hurayrah quotes the Prophet as saying: 'The best women to ride camels are the good ones among the Quraysh women: they are the most caring of children when they are young....' [Related by al-Bukhari and Muslim]

The Prophet was keen to teach women to be good carers of their children. ʿAbdullāh ibn ʿĀmir narrated: 'One day, my mother called me when the Prophet was visiting us at home. She said: "Ha, come and I shall give you...." The Prophet asked her: "What do you wish to give him?" She said: "Dates." The Prophet said to her: "If you were not to give him anything, what you said would have been recorded as a lie you said."' [Related by Abu Dāwūd]

Cooperation between husband and wife in the fulfilment of the responsibility of managing the family's affairs. Al-Aswad said: 'I asked ʿĀ'ishah what the Prophet used to do at home. She answered: "He would attend to his family's needs. When it was time for prayer, he would go out to pray."' [Related by al-Bukhari] A different version related by Ahmad mentions that ʿĀ'ishah was asked what the Prophet used to do at home. She said: 'He was an ordinary human: he checked his robe, milked his sheep and attended to his needs.' Yet another version quotes her saying: 'He stitched his robe, mended his shoes and did what men normally do at home.'

Finally, may God bless the woman who spends her day, throughout her life, caring for her children and looking after her family, like an unknown soldier seeking no publicity, but only hoping to earn God's pleasure. May God also bless the man who spends his life looking after his wife and children, ensuring that they have a comfortable living, and who is also willing to give some time to help his wife in looking after her home. Such is the attitude of a caring family man.

CHAPTER VI

The Couple's Equal Rights

- Two: Complimentary Rights
- Marriage Termination
- The man's right of divorce
- The woman's right of termination by *khul'*

Two: Complimentary Rights

The most important of these are: (1) Kind treatment; (2) Compassion; (3) Having children; (4) Trust; (5) Sharing concerns, sharing personal and general matters; (6) Good appearance; (7) Sexual enjoyment; (8) Relaxation; (9) Protective jealousy, and (10) Kindly separation.

The first of these rights of both husband and wife is kind treatment. Islam urges men to be kind to their wives, as God says: 'Consort with them in a goodly manner.' (4: 19) The Prophet said: 'The best of you are those who are best to their wives, and I am the best of you to my wives.' [Related by Ibn Mājah] The Prophet even urged the husband to offer to put a bite in his wife's mouth. Sa'd ibn Abi Waqqāṣ mentioned that the Prophet said to him: 'Whatever you spend is counted as a charity you have given, even including a bite you place in your wife's mouth....' [Related by al-Bukhari and Muslim]

Islam also urges women to be kind to their husbands. Abu Udhaynah narrated that the Prophet (peace be upon him) said: 'The best of your women is the motherly, friendly, caring and obedient, provided that they are God-fearing.' [Related by al-Bayhaqī]

The second right of both spouses is compassion, as God says: 'Among His signs is that He creates for you spouses out of your own kind, so that you might incline towards them, and He engenders love and tenderness between you. In this there are clear signs indeed for people who think.' (30: 21)

Abu Hurayrah said that God's Messenger (peace be upon him) said: 'Let no believing man hate a believing woman. If he dislikes one of her traits, he may be pleased with another,' or he might have said 'a different one.' [Related by Muslim]

The spouses' third right is having children. God says: 'God has given you spouses of your own kind and has given you, through your spouses, children and grandchildren, and provided you with wholesome sustenance.' (16: 72). Jābir mentions that the Prophet said to him: 'Jābir, seek the *kays*.' [Related by al-Bukhari and Muslim] In *Fatḥ al-Bārī*, which is a voluminous work of commentary on al-Bukhari's anthology: '*Qadi* 'Iyāḍ said that al-Bukhari and other scholars explained *kays* as the desire to have children and offspring, which is correct. The author of *al-Af'āl* mentions that when the verb is derived from this root it is attached to someone's work, and means that he does it with skill. On the other hand, al-Kisā'ī said that in such usage, it means: 'a good child has been born to him.' We should remember that God's Messenger (peace be upon him) encouraged us to have children, as he said: 'Marry a motherly and friendly woman, as I want to have the largest community.' [Related by al-Nasā'ī]

The fourth right due to both man and wife is trust. Islam urges all Muslims to trust each other and urges spouses to always think well of each other. Jābir ibn 'Abdullāh said that God's Messenger (peace be upon him) said: 'When any of you has been away from home for a long while, he should not surprise his family at night.' (Muslim's version adds: 'as though he mistrusts them or tries to find fault with them') [Related by al-Bukhari and Muslim]

Jābir ibn ʿAtīq reported that the Prophet (peace be upon him) used to say: 'Some jealousy is loved by God and some He hates. The one which God loves is that confined to real suspicion, while God dislikes jealousy when there is no reason for suspicion.' [Related by Abu Dāwūd]

The fifth right of both husband and wife is sharing concerns and sharing matters, whether personal or otherwise. The Prophet used to share his concerns with his wives. ʿĀ'ishah narrated: 'The first aspect of revelation God's Messenger (peace be upon him) received was good dreams... Then the truth was given to him as he was at Cave Ḥirā', when the angel came to him and said: "Read in the name of your Lord who created. He created man out of a clinging cell mass. Read and your Lord is the Most Bountiful one."' (96: 1-3) God's Messenger returned home with a trembling heart. He went to Khadījah bint Khuwaylid and said: "Cover me; cover me." She covered him until he calmed down. He spoke to Khadījah, telling her what happened, and said: "I fear for myself."' [Related by al-Bukhari and Muslim]

The sixth right is that both maintain a good appearance. To be keen to present oneself in a good shape is a natural human desire. There are many texts that explain that Islam urges Muslims to present themselves in good appearance. This applies to all: man and woman, young and old, rich and poor. A wise Muslim woman who seeks to draw closer to God by adorning herself, and being resourceful at that, knows how to achieve her purpose without being extravagant or time-wasting.

The Qur'an includes general evidence encouraging good appearance. This includes the order to cover what must be covered of one's body, i.e. the *ʿawrah*, and wearing good attire, particularly at the time of prayer or performing the *ṭawāf* at the Kaʿbah. God says: 'Children of Adam, dress well when you attend any place of worship. Eat and drink but do not be wasteful. Surely He does not love the wasteful.' (7: 31)

Encouraging good appearance is addressed to both men and women. ʿAbdullāh ibn Masʿūd mentions that a man said to the Prophet (peace be upon him): 'A man would like to have a fine garment and good shoes.' The Prophet said: 'God is beautiful and He loves beauty.' [Related by Muslim] ʿAbdullāh ibn Sarjis said that God's Messenger (peace be upon him) said: 'Calm consideration of matters, a moderate approach and good appearance constitute one portion out of twenty-four portions of prophethood.' [Related by al-Ṭabarānī]

Islam encourages married women to adorn themselves for their husbands. ʿAbdullāh ibn Sallām quotes the Prophet (peace be upon him): 'The best of women is the one who pleases you when you look at her.' [Related by al-Ṭabrānī] Indeed, a married woman is criticized if she abandons visible adornments: Abu Mūsā al-Ashʿarī narrated: 'ʿUthmān ibn Maẓʿūn's wife visited the Prophet's wives and they saw her in a poor condition. They said to her: 'What is wrong with you? Your husband is the richest man among the Quraysh.' She said: 'He pays no attention to me. He fasts every day and spends the night in worship.' When the Prophet came in they mentioned this to him. He then met ʿUthmān and said to him: "ʿUthmān, are you not required to follow my example?" He said: "What is it, Messenger of God?" He said: "You spend your night in worship and fast during the day. But your family has a claim on you and your body has a claim on you. Therefore, pray and sleep; and fast on and off." She visited them later wearing adornments like a bride. They asked her: "How come?" She said: "We have experienced what other people have experienced."' [Related by al-Ṭabarānī]

We learn from this hadith that using moderate makeup on one's face and hands, is perfectly appropriate for a woman in general situations.

Examples of women's adornments:

- Wearing jewellery: Ibn ʿAbbās narrated: 'God's Messenger (peace be upon him) offered two *rakʿahs* of the Eid Prayer, offering no other prayer before or after them. He then went to the women with Bilāl, and he ordered them to give *ṣadaqah*, or charity. A woman might throw in her earrings. (In a different version: a woman might give her bracelet or necklace as *ṣadaqah*.' And in yet another version: 'They threw rings of gold or silver, and other rings in Bilāl's garment'.) [Related by al-Bukhari and Muslim]

- Wearing kohl, red colouring and coloured dresses. Jābir ibn 'Abdullāh narrated: "'Alī came from Yemen with the Prophet's camels, and he found that Fāṭimah had released herself from consecration. She wore a coloured dress and applied kohl. He censured her for that. She said: "My father ordered me to do it."' [Related by Muslim]
- Muslim women attend to their makeup when their husbands return home: Jābir ibn 'Abdullāh narrated: 'We returned with the Prophet (peace be upon him) after a military expedition... When we were about to enter Madinah, he said: "Stay back so that you go home in the evening, allowing the woman with dishevelled hair to comb her hair, and the one whose husband has been away to attend to her toilet.' [Related by al-Bukhari and Muslim]
- Muslim women wear perfume before the *iḥrām* for hajj: 'Ā'ishah narrated: 'We used to come out with God's Messenger (peace be upon him) to Makkah and we would wrap on our foreheads perfumed bands. If any of us sweat, the perfume would run down her face. The Prophet might see us and he would not object.' [Related by Abu Dāwūd]

Examples of men's adornments:

- A hadith highlights several aspects of personal hygiene as well as good appearance. Needless to say, cleanliness is the essence of fine appearance. 'Ā'ishah said that the Prophet (peace be upon him) said: 'Ten things are part of sound human nature: trimming one's moustache, growing a beard, brushing teeth, inhaling water, clipping one's nails, washing finger joints, plucking armpit hair, shaving pubic hair, and washing one's bottom after defecation.' Muṣʿab [who is one of the narrators of this hadith] said: 'I forgot the tenth, but I think it is rinsing one's mouth.' [Related by Muslim]

Women's makeup of today: Every age has its own methods and tools of improving personal appearance. What methods and tools were used during the Prophet's lifetime were not sanctioned by divine revelations. They were methods people used and they were approved of by Islam. Islam approves of every method that improves appearance, provided that it does not involve anything God has forbidden. Therefore, many of the tools women use today in their makeup are acceptable for Muslim women, particularly products and powders that are applied to improve the appearance of one's eyes, cheeks, lips, hands or feet, unless their substance forms a layer that prevents water from reaching the skin when a woman performs the ablution. A basic and well-known Islamic rule is that 'things are normally permissible', unless a ruling changes this status. Therefore, it is sufficient to know what God has forbidden in this regard to realize that all else is permissible.

Forbidden makeup: 'Abdullāh ibn Masʿūd said: 'God curses the women who do tattoos and those who request it to be done for them, and the women who remove facial hair, and those who part their teeth, to appear pretty by changing God's creation. Why would I not curse the ones the Prophet cursed?' [Related by al-Bukhari and Muslim] Abu Hurayrah said that the Prophet (peace be upon him) said: 'God curses the woman who adds false hair, and the one who requests it; and also the woman who does the tattoo and the one who requests it.' [Related by al-Bukhari]

Some scholars lean towards making some exceptions regarding these ways of beautifying oneself, when they are done with the husband's consent and for his pleasure, or when they are intended as treatment for some physical defect that causes the woman physical or mental distress.

The seventh right for both husband and wife is that of sexual enjoyment. God says in the Qur'an: 'Your wives are your tilth; go, then, to your tilth as you may desire, but first provide something for your souls. Fear God and know that you shall meet Him. Give the happy news to the believers.' (2: 223)

He also says: 'They ask you about menstruation. Say: "It is an unclean condition; so keep aloof from women during menstruation, and do not draw near to them until they are cleansed. When they have cleansed themselves, you may go in unto them in the proper way, as God has bidden you. God loves those who turn to Him in repentance, and He loves those who keep themselves pure."' (2: 222)

Islam urges the woman to fulfil her husband's rights. Abu Hurayrah reports that the Prophet said: 'A woman may not fast [i.e. voluntary fasting] when her husband is present without his prior consent.' [Related by al-Bukhari and Muslim] Abu Hurayrah mentions that God's Messenger (peace be upon him) said: 'If a man calls his wife to bed, but she refuses, the angels will curse her until the morning.' [Related by Muslim]

Islam also urges the man to fulfil his wife's right. 'Awn ibn Abi Juḥayfah narrated from his father: 'The Prophet (peace be upon him) established a bond of brotherhood between Salmān and Abu al-Dardā. Salmān visited Abu al-Dardā' and he found Umm al-Dardā' wearing simple clothes. He asked her the reason and she said: 'Your brother has no desire for anything in this life.' Abu al-Dardā' came in later... Salmān said to him: "God has a claim on you, and yourself has a claim on you; and your family has a claim on you. Fulfil each one their rights." Abu al-Dardā' went to the Prophet and mentioned this to him. The Prophet said: Salmān is right.' [Related by al-Bukhari]

The proper approach to sex

- Good intention. It is good for both husband and wife to formulate the intention of maintaining their chastity, and to be satisfied with what is permissible, preferring it to anything that leads to what is foul and forbidden. God's Messenger (peace be upon him) said: '...And a charity in your intercourse.' People said: 'Messenger of God, would any of us fulfil his desire and still earn a reward for it?' The Prophet said: 'Would he not incur a sin if he does that in an unlawful way?' They said: 'Yes, he does.' The Prophet said: 'Likewise, when he does it in the lawful way, he earns a reward.' [Related by Muslim]

  It is true that the hadith mentions that the married couple are rewarded in all cases, even though they formulate no intention, because they merely do what is lawful and wholesome. However, to add to this lawful thing a good intention earns an additional reward. It is even better if the married couple also remember to thank God for His bounty in having made this lawful way available to them.
- Supplication before intercourse. Ibn 'Abbās narrated that the Prophet (peace be upon him) said: 'When a person is about to have intercourse with his wife he should say: "My Lord, keep Satan away from us and keep him away from what You give us." If he does and a child is given to them as a result, no devil shall ever harm it.' [Related by al-Bukhari]
- Purification before going to sleep. 'Abdullāh ibn Abi Qays said: 'I asked 'Ā'ishah: What did God's Messenger do when he was in a state of ceremonial impurity? Did he take a bath before going to sleep, or did he sleep before taking a bath? She said: "He did all that. He might take a bath before going to sleep, or he might perform the ablution, [i.e. *wudu*], and go to sleep." I said: All praise be to God who has left matters easy.' [Related by Muslim]

- No publicity. Sexual matters are a person's private affairs. Therefore, it is a binding duty on every Muslim man and woman not to speak to others about what they say or do when they have intercourse with their spouses. They must not reveal a defect that he or she has noticed, nor mention any private advantage which religion or social tradition require to remain private. Abu Sa'īd al-Khudrī narrated that God's Messenger (peace be upon him) said: 'One of the worst people in God's sight on the Day of Judgement is a man who is intimate with his wife and she is intimate with him, then he publicizes her secret.' [Related by Muslim]

Answering a particular question

The question is: Is it permissible for man and wife to see each other's private parts, i.e. the *'awrah*? The correct answer is that there is nothing wrong whatsoever with this. It is perfectly permissible, and it contributes to attaining maximum enjoyment, which God has made permissible to His servants. The evidence confirming this is as follows:

- Maymūnah narrated: 'I placed water for the Prophet's bath. He washed his hand twice or three times, then he poured some water on his left hand and washed his genitals. (In another version: he washed his genitals and any stains.) He then rubbed his hand on the floor, then rinsed his mouth, inhaled water, washed his face and arms, then poured water over all his body. He then changed position and washed his feet.' [Related by al-Bukhari and Muslim]
- 'Ā'ishah narrated: 'When God's Messenger (peace be upon him) wanted to take a bath, he started with his right hand, pouring water on it to wash it. He then poured water on any stains on his right hand and removed them with his left hand. Having done that, he then poured water on his head... I used to take a bath with God's Messenger, when we both were in a state

of ceremonial impurity, using the water in a single container. (In another version: using the water from a single container placed between the two of us. He would take some and I would say: Leave some for me; leave some for me.') [Related by al-Bukhari and Muslim. This is Muslim's version]

- Both Umm Salamah and Maymūnah reported that they used to take a bath with God's Messenger using the water in a single container. Their bath was to remove the state of ceremonial impurity.
- Ḥakīm narrated from his father: I said: 'Messenger of God, what may we do regarding our *'awrah*, and what we must not do?' He said: 'Keep your *'awrah* covered, except with your wife or what your right hand possesses.' [Related by Abu Dāwūd]

The eighth right of husband and wife is relaxation. Jābir ibn 'Abdullāh reports: 'My father died and left seven or nine daughters. I married a mature, previously-married woman. God's Messenger asked me: "Jābir, have you got married?" I said: "Yes." He asked: "A virgin or a mature woman?" I said: "She is a mature woman." He said: "Would it not have been better for you to marry a young one: you would play with her and she would play with you; and you would have fun together?" I said to him: "'Abdullāh has died leaving behind several daughters, and I did not want to bring them one like them. I thought it better to bring them a mature woman who would take care of them and their upbringing." He said: "May God bless you."' [Related by al-Bukhari]

The ninth right of the two spouses is protective jealousy. Islam approves of sound and healthy jealousy. Jābir ibn 'Atīq reported that the Prophet (peace be upon him) used to say: 'Some jealousy is loved by God and some He hates. The one which God loves is that confined to real suspicion, while God dislikes jealousy when there is no reason for suspicion.' [Related by Abu Dāwūd]

The tenth Right of both husband and wife is kindly separation. In his book, *Badā'i' al-Ṣanā'i'*, al-Kāsānī wrote: 'Divorce has been permitted for a benefit. A couple may have different natures and manners, and in this case the continuity of the marriage is no longer of advantage. The marriage is no longer a means to achieve purposes. Divorce becomes the benefit, because it enables each one of them to attain what they want.'

The Prophet's teachings in this area include a warning to the man against resorting to divorce and to the woman against seeking termination, i.e. *khul'*, without good and important justification or an urgent need. Ibn 'Umar said that God's Messenger (peace be upon him) said: 'The gravest of sins in the sight of God, Mighty and Exalted, is that of a man who married a woman. When he has finished his purpose with her, he divorces her and takes her dowry.' [Related by al-Ḥākim] Thawbān narrated that the Prophet (peace be upon him) said: 'A woman who asks to be divorced from her husband, without a valid reason, is forbidden even the smell of Heaven.' [Related by Abu Dāwūd]

Marriage Termination

One: The man's right of divorce

Reasons for divorce

Imam Ibn Ḥajar says: 'Divorce may be forbidden, discouraged, a duty, recommended or permissible. The first, which is forbidden, is *bid'ī*, i.e. contrary to the proper process. This may take different forms. The second, which is discouraged or *makrūh*, is the type that occurs for no reason when things between the couple are all well and proper. The third, which is a duty, applies in certain situations, such as a breach between the couple and their two arbiters agree that it is the right course of action. The fourth, which is recommended, applies when the woman is not virtuous. The fifth, which is permissible, is negated by Imam al-Nawawī. Here, other scholars cite the example of a man who is indifferent to his wife, or even dislikes her, and he is unwilling to bear her living expenses while he does not enjoy sex with her. Some scholars suggest that in such a case, divorce is not discouraged.'

Types of divorce

1. **Revocable divorce:** This allows the man to re-instate the marriage during the woman's waiting period. This is up to the husband and requires neither a new marriage contract nor a fresh dowry. However, it counts as one divorce. God says: 'Divorced women shall wait, by themselves, for three monthly courses. It is unlawful for them to conceal what God might have created in their wombs, if they believe in God and the Last Day. During this period, their husbands are entitled to take them back, if they desire reconciliation. Women shall, in all fairness, enjoy rights similar to those exercised against them, although men have an advantage over them. God is almighty, wise.' (2: 228)
2. **Complete divorce:** This occurs when the waiting period has lapsed without the re-instatement of the marriage by the husband. This type is sometimes called, 'the lesser separation.' If the couple subsequently desire to be reunited in marriage, they must have a new marriage contract and the man must pay a fresh dowry to his wife.
3. **Final divorce:** This occurs when the husband has pronounced the divorce for the third time. This type is sometimes called, 'the greater separation.' It is not permissible for the divorced husband and wife to be reunited in marriage, unless the woman has married some other man, and this other husband dies or divorces her in the normal course of events. God says: 'Divorce may be [revoked] twice, whereupon a woman may either be retained in fairness or released with kindness. It is unlawful for you to take back from women anything of what you have given them [as dowry], unless they both [husband and wife] fear that they may not be able to keep within the bounds set by God. If you have cause to fear that they would not be able to keep within the bounds set by God, it shall be no offence for either of them if she gives up whatever she may in order to free herself. These are the bounds set by God; do not, then, transgress them. Those who transgress the bounds set by God are wrongdoers indeed. Should he divorce her [a third time],

she shall not thereafter be lawful for him to remarry until she has wedded another husband. If the latter then divorces her it shall be no offence for either of the two if they return to one another, if they feel that they will be able to keep within the bounds set by God. Such are the bounds set by God. He makes them plain for people who have knowledge.' (2: 229-30)

Conditions of the validity of divorce

Condition 1

The divorce must not occur during the woman's monthly cycle, nor during a period of cleanliness from menses during which the couple had sexual intercourse. God says: 'Prophet! When you divorce women, divorce them with a view to their prescribed waiting period, and reckon the period accurately.' (65: 1) Al-Bukhari mentions this verse, then says that the divorce that complies with the Sunnah is that the man divorces his wife when she is free of menses, without having had sexual intercourse with her, and he calls in two witnesses.

ʻAbdullāh ibn ʻUmar narrated that he divorced his wife when she was in her menstruation period, during the Prophet's lifetime. ʻUmar ibn al-Khaṭṭāb asked God's Messenger (peace be upon him) about this. God's Messenger said to him: 'Order him to take her back, then to leave her until she is cleansed [from menses], then goes through another menstruation period, and is then cleansed, then he may keep her after that or divorce her before touching her.' [Related by al-Bukhari and Muslim]

Does the *bidʻī* divorce, which does not adhere to the Sunnah, take place? The fact that this type of divorce is forbidden makes clear that the divorce God has permitted is not the result of a flight of temper, or a decision taken at a moment of extreme reaction. It must be a decision with profound and well-considered reasons. It is not a decision that is changed because of waiting for a period of cleanliness from menses during which no sexual intercourse has taken place between the spouses.

Condition 2

The three divorces must not be combined on the same occasion. God says: 'Divorced women shall wait, by themselves, for three monthly courses. It is unlawful for them to conceal what God might have created in their wombs, if they believe in God and the Last Day. During this period, their husbands are entitled to take them back, if they desire reconciliation. Women shall, in all fairness, enjoy rights similar to those exercised against them, although men have an advantage over them. God is Almighty, Wise. Divorce may be [revoked] twice, whereupon a woman may either be retained in fairness or released with kindness.' (2: 228-9)

Ibn 'Abbās said: 'During the time of God's Messenger (peace be upon him), Abu Bakr and the first two years of 'Umar's reign, three utterances of divorce counted as one divorce. 'Umar ibn al-Kaṭṭāb then said: "People are precipitating something in which they have been given respite. We better commit them to it." He imposed it on them.' [Related by Muslim]

Divorce after the exchange of mutual cursing is an exception from this condition. Sahl ibn Sa'd al-Sā'idī narrated: '... 'Uwaymir went over to God's Messenger as people were around him. He said:

3. The exchange of mutual curses refers to a situation when a man accuses his wife of adultery and has no witnesses to support the accusation. He is required to state his accusation under oath five times and couple the fifth oath with invoking God's curse on himself if he is telling a lie. The woman is then given the choice of stating five times under oath that he is making a false accusation, coupling the fifth oath with invoking God's wrath on herself if his accusation is true. If both exchange these oaths, with the invocation of God's curse and wrath, their marriage is absolutely terminated forever, with no possibility of reunion, and neither is punished.

"Messenger of God, suppose that a man finds his wife with a man: should he kill him and then you kill him [in return]? Or what shall he do?" God's Messenger (peace be upon him) said: "Revelation has been given concerning you and your wife. Go and bring her." Sahl said: They exchanged curses. I was with the people attending God's Messenger (peace be upon him). When they had done so, 'Uwaymir said: "Messenger of God, if I retain her as my wife, I would have told a lie against her." He divorced her three times before God's Messenger (peace be upon him) ordered him. Ibn Shihāb said: Such was the case of the couple exchanging curses.'

Imam ibn Ḥajar said: 'The statement, "He divorced her three times before God's Messenger (peace be upon him) ordered him," has been questioned, as scholars say that the termination of the marriage in the case of mutual curses between man and wife takes place by the very act of exchanging curses.' It is possible to say that the Prophet did not blame 'Uwaymir for divorcing his wife three times together, either because the final termination of the marriage had occurred by the exchange of curses, and his divorce became meaningless, or because combining three divorces is applicable only in this situation.

Condition 3

The divorce should be with a clear intention, not a mere thought or contemplation. It must not be in a situation of extreme anger when one does not realize what one is saying, nor in a situation of unintentional mistake, or forgetfulness, compulsion, drunkenness or madness.

- Clear intention. 'Umar ibn al-Khaṭṭāb said that God's Messenger (peace be upon him) said: 'Actions are but by intention. Everyone shall have only that which they have intended.' [Related by al-Bukhari and Muslim]
- It must not be a mere thought. Abu Hurayrah reports that the Prophet (peace be upon him) said: 'God overlooks what

my community entertains of thoughts, as long as they do not act on it or express it in words.' [Related by al-Bukhari and Muslim]

- It must not be in a situation of mental closure, i.e. extreme anger. 'Ā'ishah narrated that God's Messenger (peace be upon him) said: 'No divorce or slave freeing occurs in a flight of extreme anger.' [Related by Ibn Mājah]
- It must not be in a situation of unintentional mistake, or forgetfulness, or compulsion. Abu Dharr al-Ghifārī said that God's Messenger (peace be upon him) said: 'God does not hold my community to account for what they do by mistake or through forgetfulness or under compulsion.' [Related by Ibn Mājah]
- It must not be done under the influence of drink. 'Alī reports that he said: 'Messenger of God, I have never had a day like this. Ḥamzah attacked my two camels, cutting off their humps and stabbed them in their waists. He is now in a home drinking with some people.' The Prophet called for his upper garment and put it on then went out... The Prophet spoke to Ḥamzah, blaming him for what he did, but Ḥamzah was drunk, and his eyes were red. He looked at the Prophet then said: 'Are you not but my father's slaves?' The Prophet realized that he was totally drunk. God's Messenger then retreated, going backward. He left and we left with him. [Related by al-Bukhari and Muslim]
- It must not be in a situation of madness. 'Alī mentions that the Prophet said: 'Accountability does not apply to three types of person: the one who is asleep until he wakes up, a child until it has attained puberty, and a mad person until he has regained his mental faculties. (In another version: the weak-minded until he has recovered).' [Related by Abu Dāwūd]

Condition 4

The divorce must not be conditional, i.e. dependent on something that is done or left undone. Imam Ibn Taymiyyah said:

> Speech that is said in cases of divorce is of three types: enforceable, supported by oath and conditional. The enforceable formula is to pronounce the divorce without tying it to any situation or oath. This is when a man says to his wife: 'You are divorced,' or 'so-and-so is divorced,' or words to this effect. This type is called 'enforceable.'
>
> The 'oath formula' is when a man says: 'My wife is divorced unless I do this, or I abandon that.' This is an oath to urge himself or someone else to do or to stop doing something, or to believe or disbelieve something. This type is considered under questions of divorce and oaths. According to all linguists, this formula is an oath. Fiqh scholars also agree that it is an oath formula. They do not differ on this point, but they differ in their rulings. Some scholars lean towards the divorce aspect, ruling that the divorce occurs if the oath is broken. Other scholars lean towards the oath aspect, saying that the divorce does not occur, but the man incurs an oath atonement if he breaks his oath. Some do not even require such atonement.
>
> The 'conditional formula' is when the man says to his wife something like: 'If you do such-and-such, you are divorced.' This type is also called 'situational divorce.' In this case, the man either intends his words as an oath and does not really want to divorce his wife even if the situation occurs, or he intends the divorce to take place if the situation occurs and the condition is met. The first case is given the same ruling as the oath formula, and this is agreed by all scholars... In the second case, which means

that the man intended the divorce when the situation occurs, the divorce takes place when the condition is met, in the same way as the 'enforceable' type occurs according to the general agreement of early and later scholars. The same applies to a divorce attached to a particular time, such as a man saying to his wife: 'You are divorced on the first day of next month.'

Manners to be observed at the time of divorce

1. **Kindly separation.** This means to be gentle with the divorced woman and to treat her with kindness. God says: 'Divorce may be [revoked] twice, whereupon a woman may either be retained in fairness or released with kindness.' (2: 229) 'When you have divorced women and they have reached the end of their waiting-term, either retain them with fairness or let them go with fairness.' (2: 231) 'Prophet! Say to your wives: "If you desire the life of this world and its charms, I shall provide for you and release you in a becoming manner."' (33: 28)

   One aspect of kindness is not to confront one's wife with the clear word of divorce. Al-Bukhari opens a chapter with the heading: 'Should a man confront a woman with divorce?' He then mentions the following hadith: ''Ā'ishah reported that when al-Jawn's daughter was admitted into the Prophet's presence and he drew close to her, she said: "I seek shelter with God from you." He said to her: "You seek the shelter with the Great One. You re-join your family." (In another version: 'He said: "You seek the shelter with the One who extends it," and he left... He said

---

4. Al-Jawn's daughter was a Bedouin woman offered by her people to the Prophet as a wife and he accepted. However, someone told her that she should say to him these words when they first met. She did this and the Prophet divorced her without consummating the marriage.

[to her relative]: Abu Usayd, give her two long lace garments and sent her back to her people).' [Related by al-Bukhari]

2. **Witnesses for divorce and the reinstatement of the marriage:** God says: 'When they have completed their appointed term, either retain them in fair manner or part with them in fair manner. Call to witness two people of known probity from among yourselves; and do yourselves bear witness before God. Thus is admonished everyone who believes in God and the Last Day. For everyone who fears God, He will grant a way out.' (65: 2)
3. **A generous gift is required:** God says: 'You will incur no sin if you divorce women before having touched them or settled a dowry for them. Provide for them, the rich according to his means and the straitened according to his means. Such a provision, in an equitable manner, is an obligation binding on the righteous.' (2: 236) 'Divorced women shall have a provision according to what is fair. This is an obligation on the God-fearing.' (2: 241) He also said: 'Prophet! Say to your wives: "If you desire the life of this world and its charms, I shall provide for you and release you in a becoming manner."' (33: 28)
4. **Both parties are recommended to act generously when divorce occurs before consummation:** God says: 'If you divorce them before having touched them but after having settled a dowry for them, then give them half of that which you have settled, unless they forgo it or he in whose hand is the marriage tie forgoes it. To forgo what is due to you is closer to being righteous. Do not forget to act benevolently to one another. God sees all that you do.' (2: 237) 'Forgoing' in this case means that the woman should forgo her entitlement to half the agreed dowry, partially or totally, and it also means that the man should give her more than what he owes her.
5. **The divorced woman's right to breastfeed her children and take care of them:** God says: 'Mothers may breast-feed their children for two whole years; [that is] for those who wish to complete the suckling. The father of the child is responsible to provide in a

fair manner for their sustenance and clothing. No human being shall be burdened with more than he is well able to bear. Neither shall a mother be allowed to cause her child to suffer, nor shall a father cause suffering to his child. The same shall apply to the father's heir. If, by mutual consent and after due consultation, the parents choose to wean the child, they will incur no sin thereby. Nor shall it be any offence on your part if you engage wet nurses for your children, provided that you hand over what you agreed to pay, in a fair manner. Fear God, and know that God sees all that you do.' (2: 233)

Imam Ibn Ḥajar quotes Ibn Baṭṭāl: 'All scholars agree that the wages for breastfeeding a child are borne by the husband, after the divorced woman has finished her waiting period. When the divorce is complete, the child's mother is more entitled to breastfeed her child.' 'Abdullāh ibn 'Amr said that a woman came and said: 'Messenger of God, this son of mine: he grew in my tummy and was fed from my breast. My lap was his caring place. His father has divorced me and now he wants to take him away from me.' The Prophet said to her: 'You are more entitled to him unless you get married.' [Related by Abu Dāwūd]

One aspect of the kind treatment God ordered a husband to extend to his divorcee is that her allowance for looking after the child remains at the same standard of living she used to have before the divorce, as long as he can afford it.

6. **The waiting period:**

   - Duration: For women who go through the normal monthly cycle, God says: 'Divorced women shall wait, by themselves, for three monthly courses.' (2: 228) As for women who are past the menopause or those who do not have such courses, God says: 'As for those of your women who are beyond the age of monthly courses, as well as for those who do not have any courses, their waiting period, if you have any doubt, is three months.' (65: 4) A pregnant woman who is divorced continues her waiting period until she has given birth. God says: 'As for those who are with child, their waiting term shall end when they deliver their burden.' (65: 4) This means that once the pregnancy is over, either through abortion or childbirth, the woman's waiting period is finished.

- A woman who is divorced before the consummation of her marriage is exempt from observing a waiting period. God says: 'Believers! If you marry believing women and then divorce them before the marriage is consummated, you have no reason to expect them to observe a waiting period. Hence, provide well for them and release them in a becoming manner.' (33: 49)
- Making sure of the beginning of the waiting period. God says: 'Prophet! When you divorce women, divorce them with a view to their prescribed waiting period, and reckon the period accurately.' (65: 1) Imam Ibn Ḥajar said that the order to 'reckon the period accurately' means making sure of the day when the waiting period begins, so that the matter is not confused, leading to greater pressure on the divorced woman.
- During her waiting period, a divorcee stays in her marital home. God says: 'Prophet! When you divorce women, divorce them with a view to their prescribed waiting period, and reckon the period accurately. Be conscious of God, your Lord. Do not drive them out of their homes, nor shall they themselves leave, unless they commit a flagrant indecency. These are the bounds set by God. Whoever transgresses God's bounds wrongs his own soul. You never know; after that, God may bring about some new situation.' (65: 1)

5. The plural form is used here indicating that the address is to the Muslim community as a whole.

- Fāṭimah bint Qays said to those who argued with her: 'The final say between us is the Qur'an, and God says: "Be conscious of God, your Lord. Do not drive them out of their homes, nor shall they themselves leave, unless they commit a flagrant indecency. These are the bounds set by God. Whoever transgresses God's bounds wrongs his own soul. You never know; after that, God may bring about some new situation." (65: 1) This applies when a re-instatement of the marriage is possible. What can happen after a third divorce? Why would you impose restrictions on the woman?' [Related by Muslim]

In the light of this hadith, the weightier opinion is that in the case of a revocable divorce, the woman must spend her waiting period in her marital home, which provides an opportunity for reconciliation and re-instatement of the marriage. A woman whose divorce is final, having gone through three divorces, leaves her husband's home because she cannot be reunited with him in marriage until she has gone through a normal marriage with a different husband.

- During her waiting period, a divorcee stays at home, going out only for a legitimate reason. God says: 'Nor shall they themselves leave.' (65: 1).

Jābir ibn 'Abdullāh reports: 'My aunt was divorced. She wanted to go and have her dates gathered. A man reproached her for wanting to go out. She went to the Prophet and told him. He said to her: "Yes, you can gather your fruit. It may be that you will give something as charity or do some other good work."' [Related by Muslim]

- The husband bears the woman's expenses during her waiting period. Separation with kindness, which is ordered by God, means that her expenses should be at the same level the woman had during her marriage, prior to being divorced, as long as this continues to be within the husband's means.

- A woman is in trust of what she might have conceived. God says: 'Divorced women shall wait, by themselves, for three monthly courses. It is unlawful for them to conceal what God might have created in their wombs, if they believe in God and the Last Day.' (2: 228)
- No express proposal during a woman's waiting period is permitted, but a hint is allowed when the divorce is final. God says: 'You will incur no sin if you give a hint of a marriage offer to [widowed] women or keep such an intention to yourselves. God knows that you will entertain such intentions concerning them. Do not, however, plight your troth in secret; but speak only in a decent manner. Furthermore, do not resolve on actually making the marriage tie before the prescribed term [of waiting] has run its course. Know well that God knows what is in your minds, so have fear of Him; and know that God is much-forgiving, clement.' (2: 235)

Fāṭimah bint Qays reports: 'My husband Abu 'Amr ibn Ḥafṣ ibn al-Mughīrah sent me 'Ayyash ibn Abi Rabī'ah to inform me that he had divorced me. He sent with him five *ṣā's* of dates and five of barley. [The *ṣā'* was a measure equal to a little more than two kilograms] I said to him: Is this all my maintenance? Am I not to observe my waiting period in your home? He said: "No." I put on my clothes and went to see the Prophet. He asked me how many times I was divorced. I said: three. He said: "He is right. You cannot claim maintenance. You can observe your waiting period at your cousin's home, Ibn Umm Maktūm. Since he is a blind man, you can take off your top garments in his home. When you finish your waiting period, let me know."' [Related by Muslim] Another version of this hadith mentions that the Prophet sent her a word telling her not to get married without letting him know.

Al-Nawawī said that 'the hadith makes clear that it is permissible to give a hint of one's intention to propose to a woman observing her waiting period if her divorce is final. This is the correct view of our Shāfiʿī School.' We may add here that the hint given to Fāṭimah by the Prophet was because he wanted her to marry Usāmah ibn Zayd, a favourite of his.

7. **Thinking well of divorced women and offering to marry them:** God says: 'Then, when Zayd had come to the end of his union with her, We gave her to you in marriage, so that no blame should attach to the believers for marrying the spouses of their adopted sons when the latter have come to the end of their union with them. God's will must be fulfilled.' (33: 37)
8. **Guardians should welcome reconciliation after divorce:** God says: 'And when you have divorced women and they have reached the end of their waiting-term, do not prevent them from marrying their husbands if they have agreed with each other in a fair manner. This is an admonition for everyone of you who believes in God and the Last Day. That is more virtuous for you, and purer. God knows, whereas you do not know.' (2: 232)

Proposed regulation of divorce

The following regulatory steps are suggested:

- A legal requirement that divorce must be registered with a judge.
- When a judge receives a request to register a divorce, he refers the request to two arbiters, one from the relatives of each spouse, so that the arbiters try to achieve reconciliation. This is in implementation of the Qur'anic verse, as God says: 'If you have reason to fear that a breach may occur between a [married] couple, appoint an arbiter from among his people and an arbiter from among her people. If they both want to set things aright, God will bring about their reconciliation. God is indeed all knowing, aware of all things.' (4: 35)
- If the husband has submitted the request to register the divorce when he intended to divorce his wife but before actually

going through with it by clear pronunciation, and the two arbiters are successful in achieving reconciliation, the husband withdraws his request of registration.

- If the husband has actually initiated the divorce by clear pronunciation of it before submitting the request to register it, and then the two arbiters are successful, bringing about reconciliation, this means a return to normal family life. In this case, the judge looks into the divorce as it was done. If it meets the conditions of a correct divorce, he records it as having happened. If it does not meet these conditions, he refuses to record it.
- Likewise, the judge has to establish that the conditions of valid divorce are met, if the two arbiters fail to achieve reconciliation. The divorce is recorded only if it meets the conditions of validity.
- The media should explain that men must not resort to actually pronouncing the divorce before resorting to the court, which may be able to achieve an amicable solution to the family problem. This means that since there is an obligatory step of attempting reconciliation before recording the divorce, then there is no need to actually resort to it before going through this attempt.

Two: The woman's right of termination by *khul'* is the same as the man's right of divorce

God says in the Qur'an: 'It is unlawful for you to take back from women anything of what you have given them [as dowry], unless they both [husband and wife] fear that they may not be able to keep within the bounds set by God. If you have cause to fear that they would not be able to keep within the bounds set by God, it shall be no offence for either of them if she gives up whatever she may in order to free herself. These are the bounds set by God; do not, then, transgress them. Those who transgress the bounds set by God are wrongdoers indeed.' (2: 229)

Ibn ʿAbbās reports: "Thābit ibn Qays's wife came to the Prophet and said: 'Messenger of God! I do not take anything against Thābit, either with regard to his faith or manners, but I am worried lest I should be ungrateful.' (In another version, she said: 'I do not blame Thābit in regard to his faith or manners, but I dislike him.') The Prophet asked her: 'Are you prepared to give him back his garden?' She said: 'Yes,' and she returned his garden to him. The Prophet ordered him to leave her." [Related by al-Bukhari]

How does the *khulʿ* occur? The proper way is that it is by an agreement between the man and his wife. If the husband does not accept what the woman gives up to free herself, she submits a request to a judge.

Khulʿ has two scenarios: the real one is when the husband is blameless, but the wife dislikes him and wants to be released from her marriage. The other scenario is when the husband ill-treats his wife, but she cannot prove the harm he causes her and permits divorce. Therefore, she requests *khulʿ* and buys her own freedom by returning to him what he had paid her in dowry. In this case, the husband incurs the sin of taking such payment unlawfully.

The amount of payment

In *Fatḥ al-Bārī*, Ibn Ḥajar quotes Ibn Baṭṭāl: 'The majority of scholars are of the view that it is permissible for a husband to take more than the dowry he had paid his wife. Mālik said that he never met any scholar of note who disallows this, but it does not reflect a character of high moral values... He cites the hadith in support of the view that the payment for releasing the woman is either the dowry itself or its value, because the Prophet asked the woman: Are you prepared to

6. The garden was the dowry her husband gave her at the time of the marriage. When a woman wants to terminate her marriage, through what is known as *khulʿ*, she refunds him any dowry he had given her.

give him back his garden? In the version related by Ibn Mājah and al-Bayhaqī, the hadith concludes with: The Prophet ordered him to take it back but nothing more.'

Regulating the **khul'**

We suggest regulating the *khul'* as we did with divorce. In brief, if the couple agree to the *khul'*, they are required to register the termination of the marriage by *khul'* with a judge. The judge then refers the request of registration to two arbiters from the relatives of the husband and wife, who will attempt to achieve reconciliation. The termination of the marriage will not be recorded until the arbiters declare their failure to achieve reconciliation.

CHAPTER VII

Dealing with Marital Disagreements

Features of marital disagreements

We said that a family has special features in the way it is formed and by virtue of its objectives, distinguishing it from all other institutions. It stands to reason, then, that disagreements between husband and wife should have special features with regard to their nature or the measures needed to sort such out.

- Abu Hurayrah said that the Prophet said: 'Take good care of women.'
- Ibn 'Abbās reports that the Prophet (peace be upon him) said: 'I was shown Hell and I found that women are the majority of its dwellers, because they are ungrateful.' People asked: 'Do they disbelieve in God?' He said: 'They are ungrateful to their partners and ungrateful for kindness. You may be kind to

a woman for a very long time, then she is displeased with something you do and she says: "I never had anything good from you."' [Related by al-Bukhari and Muslim]

- Abu al-Dardā' said that God's Messenger (peace be upon him) said: 'Shall I tell of a grade that is better than fasting, prayer and *ṣadaqah*?' People said: 'Yes, please.' He said: 'Maintaining strong ties [with relatives and within the community]. The severance of ties is catastrophic.' [Related by al-Tirmidhī]
- Jābir said: 'God's Messenger (peace be upon him) said: "Iblīs takes his throne on the sea. He sends his troops to lead people astray. The best of them in his eyes is the one who leads farthest astray. One of them comes and says I have done this and that. He [i.e. Satan] says: "You have done very little." Then another one comes and says: "I did not leave this man until I had caused a schism between him and his wife." He brings him close to himself and says: "Splendid you are."' [Related by Muslim]

Disagreement between a man and wife is unlike a quarrel between any other two Muslims. It is a type of the worst evil. Hence, Satan is delighted with it, as clearly stated in the last hadith. God's Messenger (peace be upon him) gives a strong warning against saying anything that leads to disagreement between man and wife. Abu Hurayrah mentions that the Prophet said: 'A person who spoils relations between a woman and her husband does not belong to us.' [Related by Abu Dāwūd] Therefore, a Muslim couple must always guard against the great evil to which their disagreement leads. They should seek God's shelter against Satan's promptings allowing him no chance to perpetrate an act of great evil through them. Both husband and wife should remember the Prophet's advice which we mentioned in connection of both spouses' right of compassion: Abu Hurayrah said that God's Messenger (peace be upon him) said: 'Let no believing man hate a believing woman. If he dislikes one of her traits, he may be pleased with another', or he might have said 'a different one.' [Related by Muslim] Although this hadith seems to address the husband, it is equally applicable to the wife.

Remarriage after divorce

If the divorce is revocable: God says: 'During this period, their husbands are entitled to take them back, if they desire reconciliation.' (2: 228) 'Umar mentioned that God's Messenger (peace be upon him) divorced Ḥafṣah, then reinstated his marriage to her.' [Related by Abu Dāwūd] Ibn 'Abbās reported: 'Rukānah ibn 'Abd Yazīd divorced his wife three times on the same occasion. He was extremely sorry for doing so. The Prophet (peace be upon him) asked him: "How did you divorce her?" He said: "Three times in one sitting." The Prophet said: "This is only one divorce. You may take her back if you wish." Rukānah took his wife back.' [Related by Ahmad]

If the divorce is complete, i.e. with the woman's waiting period having lapsed, remarriage requires a fresh contract and the payment of a new dowry. God says: 'And when you have divorced women and they have reached the end of their waiting-term, do not prevent them from marrying their husbands if they have agreed with each other in a fair manner. This is an admonition for everyone of you who believes in God and the Last Day. That is more virtuous for you, and purer. God knows, whereas you do not know.' (2: 232)

If the divorce is final, i.e. having occurred three times, the couple cannot be reunited in marriage until the woman has gone through a normal marriage with a different husband. God says: 'Should he divorce her [a third time], she shall not thereafter be lawful for him to remarry until she has wedded another husband. If the latter then divorces her it shall be no offence for either of the two if they return to one another, if they feel that they will be able to keep within the bounds set by God.' (2: 230)

ʿĀ'ishah, the Prophet's wife, said: 'Rifāʿah al-Quraẓī's [former] wife came to the Prophet (peace be upon him). She said: "I was with Rifāʿah and he divorced me, making my divorce final. I married ʿAbd al-Raḥmān ibn al-Zabīr. What he has is just like the edge of a robe." God's Messenger (peace be upon him) smiled and said: "Do you want to go back to Rifāʿah? No way; until you have experienced his [i.e. ʿAbd al-Raḥmān's] sweetness and he experienced yours."' [Related by al-Bukhari and Muslim]

This is a situation of a woman who wants to go back to her former husband who has divorced her three times. Another case mentions a man's desire to be reunited with his former wife. Nāfiʿ, ʿAbdullāh ibn ʿUmar's *mawlā*, reported that a man said to Ibn ʿUmar: 'My maternal uncle divorced his wife, and he was distressed and the matter became too hard for him. I want to marry her. He did not ask me; nor does he know of it.' Ibn ʿUmar said: 'No, unless it is a proper marriage: if you like her, you retain her; and if you dislike her, you divorce her. Otherwise, in God's Messenger's lifetime we used to consider this a case of sinful fornication.' [Related by al-Ṭabarānī]

Degrees of disagreement and methods of solution

We start by saying that 'prevention is better than cure.' Certain measures are very useful in ensuring such prevention. The first measure is the fulfilment of the duties of companionship. Secondly, being tolerant and overlooking minor shortcomings and shortfalls. Another important measure is to be alert to the early indications of an approaching disagreement.

The first and easiest degree of disagreement is common to every family, because a family is composed of human beings, not angels. Human weakness must lead to some minor and repeated slipages or occasional serious ones. Examples of such easy disagreement are shown in the following hadiths:

Anas narrated that the Prophet (peace be upon him) was with one of his wives, when another Mother of the Believers sent him a plate of food. His wife in whose home the Prophet was hit the servant bringing the food on his hand and he dropped the food causing the plate to break. The Prophet gathered the pieces of the plate and picked up the food placing it on it. He said: 'Your mother has been jealous.' He retained the servant, then brought a plate from the home he was in. He sent the sound plate to his wife whose plate was broken and kept the broken plate where it was broken.' [Related by al-Bukhari]

'Ā'ishah reports: 'God's Messenger (peace be upon him) once said to me: "I know when you are happy with me and when you are angry with me." I asked: How do you know that? He said: "When you are happy with me you say: 'Yes indeed, by the Lord of Muhammad.' When you are angry with me you would say: 'No, by the Lord of Abraham'." I said: "This is true. I only stop using your name."' [Related by al-Bukhari and Muslim]

The second degree of disagreement is that which concerns some important matter that is not easy to overlook. In such a case, more effective measures are needed to overcome the disagreement. These may include:

- Bringing in a relative or a friend as an intermediary. One example of such a measure is given in the following hadith:

  Jābir ibn 'Abdullāh narrated: 'Abu Bakr came over, seeking permission to enter the Prophet's home, and he found people seated at his door. None was given permission to enter. However, Abu Bakr was permitted and he went in. Then 'Umar came over, sought permission and it was granted. He found the Prophet seated with his wives around him, but he looked gloomy and he was silent. Abu Bakr thought: I shall say something to make the Prophet laugh. He said:

"Messenger of God, I wish you had seen Bint Khārijah [his wife] when she asked me for more money. I went up to her and poked her in the neck." God's Messenger smiled and said: "They are here around me as you see, asking me for more money." Abu Bakr went up to 'Ā'ishah to poke her in the neck and 'Umar went up to Ḥafṣah to poke her in the neck. Both said: "You are asking God's Messenger (peace be upon him) what he does not have?" They said: "By God, we never ask God's Messenger (peace be upon him) something he does not have." [Related by Muslim]

- Forgoing some of one's rights

God says: 'If a woman has reason to fear ill-treatment or desertion by her husband, it shall not be wrong for the two of them if they should try to set things peacefully to rights between them; for peace is best. Avarice is ever-present in human souls. If you act with kindness and are God-fearing, surely God is aware of all that you do.' (4: 128)

- Staying away for some time

An example of this is what happened between God's Messenger and his wives when they disagreed over the question of family expenses. The Prophet needed to stay away from his wives for a whole month. Both Abu Bakr and 'Umar intervened first, but this did not sort out the problem. This period of separation was very hard on the Prophet himself, his wives and the Muslim community generally.

- Arbitration

When disagreement continues and aggravates, with none of the aforementioned methods being effective, the married couple, or some person of authority, resort to arbitration, which is mentioned in the following Qur'anic verse: 'If you have reason to fear that a breach may occur between a [married] couple, appoint an arbiter from among his people and an arbiter from among her people. If they both want to set things aright, God will bring about their reconciliation. God is indeed all knowing, aware of all things.' (4: 35)

The permission to use physical discipline in cases of rebellion

God says: 'As for those women from whom you have reason to fear rebellion, admonish them [first]; then leave them alone in bed; then hit them. Then, if they pay you heed, do not seek any pretext to harm them. God is indeed most high, great.' (4: 34) This verse shows that a physical disciplinary measure is allowed, but we also have several other texts that urge Muslims not to resort to it.

---

7. In most, if not all, translations of the Qur'an, the phrase *waḍribūhunn* is rendered 'and beat them.' I am using here, 'and hit them', because it is slightly less harsh and reflects the author's understanding. However, I do not feel that this reflects the intended meaning. According to the *Cambridge English Dictionary*, beat is defined as 'to hit someone repeatedly.' In other dictionaries an intention to cause pain or injury is added. This is definitely different from what the measure recommended in this verse means. Nor do we find in English a synonym or analogous word that fits the context. Therefore, we need to explain the recommended measure. To do so, we must, of necessity, resort to the Prophet's own guidance and the linguistic usage of the word.

    1. As regards the Prophet's own action, we have the hadith narrated by 'Ā'ishah and quoted by the author: 'God's Messenger never beat anyone with his hand, not a woman, not a servant, except when he fought for God's cause.' When a maid angered him, he said to her: 'Had it not been for my fear of God, I would have punished you with this toothbrush.' When his wives jointly pressurised him for a more comfortable living, he admonished them, and when the admonition did not work, he stayed away from them for a month. He then gave them a free choice: either to remain with him or to be divorced in an amicable and honourable way. They all chose to stay with him. Moreover, he continually stressed that a man who

'Ā'ishah narrated: 'God's Messenger (peace be upon him) never hit anything with his hand, nor ever hit a woman or a servant. Nor did he ever avenge himself when he was subjected to harm. Only when he fought for God's sake [did he hit his enemies] or if some violation of God's prohibition was committed, [then] he exacted punishment, for God's sake.' [Related by Muslim]

Iyās ibn 'Abdullāh said: God's Messenger (peace be upon him) said: 'Do not beat God's female servants.' 'Umar later came to the Prophet and said: 'Women have become undisciplined.' The Prophet gave a concession allowing men to hit them. Many women visited the

---

beats his wife is not a good person and counselled his Companions and his followers never to resort to such measures.

2. The Arabic root *ḍarb* is used in the Qur'an in various forms 17 times. Few of these are intended in the sense of hitting, and one or two carry different senses, but the sense that is clear in most instances is that of 'separation, isolation, abandoning, staying away from, etc..' The question that arises here is in which sense is the word used in this verse?

Essentially, this verse and the following one mention four different measures to be resorted to in cases of rebellion that threatens the continuity of marriage. These measures are meant to provide a gradual course which means that they have to be followed in sequence, not as alternatives available all the time. In other words, admonition is the first step. Only when it is not heeded may the next measure of using separate beds be resorted to. The third measure is the one we are trying to understand. The fourth, which is stated in the next verse, is to refer the matter for arbitration by a relative of each of the couple. The two arbiters should try to work out reconciliation between man and wife. Thus, we have three measures resorted to within the family home, with no interference by even close relatives, while the fourth seeks reconciliation with the help of relatives. Could this come about after the man had beaten his wife? Would the beating not have forestalled the efforts of arbiters? In other words, any such beating would have polarized the situation and made both parties stick to their original stances.

Looking at all these factors, I concur with the view that the phrase *wa-ḍribūhunn* is used here in the sense of separation, rather than any physical punishment. This separation means that the husband stays away from the family home for a few days, so as to give a chance for tempers to cool down and both husband and wife to think about their situation in a cooler and wiser way.

Prophet's family complaining about their husbands. The Prophet said: 'Many women visited Muhammad's family complaining about their husbands. Those are not your good men.' [Related by Abu Dāwūd]

This and many other hadiths show that physical discipline may only be resorted to when there is some urgent need coupled with the hope that it will achieve useful results. Such results are subject to the local social environment and the mental and moral standard of both the one who resorts to this method and its recipient. It is indeed a measure to which the old Arabian proverb applies: 'The last type of medicine is cauterization.'

Urging all people not to resort to physical punishment, the Legislator, in His infinite wisdom, put in place certain requirements to reduce its severity, when the situation makes its use necessary.

1. Beating must be gentle. ʿAbdullāh ibn Zamʿah narrated that he heard the Prophet addressing the people... 'He mentioned women and admonished men in their treatment. He said: "Any of you may whip his wife as he would whip his slave. Yet he may take her to bed at the end of the day!."' Another version quotes the Prophet: 'Why would any of you beat his wife like he beats his mount? He may later hug her.' [Related by al-Bukhari and Muslim]
2. Not on the face. Muʿāwiyah ibn Ḥaydah said that he asked God's Messenger (peace be upon him): 'What right has a wife against her husband?' He said: 'That you feed her when you eat, give her clothing when you have some (or when you have earned some money). That you do not slap her on the face, hurl verbal abuse or stay away, except at home.' [Related by Abu Dāwūd]
3. Intercession. To intercede in a difficult situation hoping to bring a good result is encouraged by Islam. It is definitely

good to help a Muslim to keep his reaction under control and to refrain from what Islam forbids of verbal abuse and painful beating. The hadith that says, 'A man may not be asked for what reason he has beaten his wife,' is unauthentic.

The third degree of disagreement between a married couple is the hardest. Here are some examples of this degree:

One party feels a strong dislike towards the other, to the extent that they do not wish to continue with the marriage. This is what was expressed by Thābit ibn Qays's wife when she asked the Prophet for the termination of her marriage. Ibn ʿAbbās reports: 'Thābit ibn Qays's wife came to the Prophet and said: "Messenger of God! I do not take anything against Thābit, either with regard to his faith or manners, but I am worried lest I should be ungrateful." (In another version, she said: "but I dislike him.") The Prophet asked her: "Are you prepared to give him back his garden?" She said: 'Yes,' and she returned his garden to him. The Prophet ordered him to leave her.' [Related by al-Bukhari]

One party discovers a deep-rooted moral weakness in the other, which colours that party's general conduct. Yet that party does not admit that it is unbecoming. Ibn ʿAbbās narrated that a man said to the Prophet: 'Messenger of God, I am married to a woman who does not repel the hand of anyone who touches her.' The Prophet said to him: 'Divorce her.' The man said: 'But I love her.' [Related by al-Nasā'ī]

One party is guilty of adultery. Sahl ibn Saʿd narrated that an Anṣārī man said: 'Messenger of God, suppose that a man finds his wife with

---

8. Some women like to show off. If a man looks at such a woman or touches her, she does not show any displeasure. Marriage to such a woman is discouraged. This is why the Prophet advised the man in this case to divorce his wife, but he did not order him to do so when the man said that he loved her. - Author's note.

a man: should he kill him and then you kill him [in return]? Or what shall he do?' God's Messenger (peace be upon him) said: "Revelation has been given concerning you and your wife. Go and bring her." Sahl said: They exchanged curses. I was with the people attending God's Messenger (peace be upon him). When they had done so, the man said: "Messenger of God, if I retain her as my wife, I would have told a lie against her." He divorced her three times before God's Messenger (peace be upon him) ordered him. He parted with her when they were still with the Prophet (peace be upon him).' [Related by al-Bukhari and Muslim]

When disagreement between man and wife has reached this level, there is no option but to terminate the marriage either by divorce or *khul'*.

CHAPTER VIII

More than One Wife

God says: 'You may marry of other women as may be agreeable to you, two or three or four. But if you fear that you will not be able to maintain fairness between them, then marry only one.' (4: 3) What Islam says is: 'You may marry of other women as may be agreeable to you.' What is meant by 'agreeable to you' is what will be good for you and will set your affairs on the right course. This refers to the affairs of the man, his wives and children, because when the man's affairs are set right, those around him will feel that their affairs are also on the right course. Likewise, we think that when the affairs of one's wives and children are on the wrong course, one is not in a healthy condition and he has worries to deal with.

The purpose of permitting polygamy is, then, to ensure that the family is in a good condition. It is definitely not intended just for the mere pleasure of the man. If a man needs to have more than one wife, so as to ensure that his affairs are well, yet he is prevented from marrying more than one, then he will be at a disadvantage.

His activity will weaken and his comfort will reduce, in proportion to the importance of that need. Inevitably, his condition will also have an adverse effect on the family as a whole.

By contrast, if a man's fine condition requires having one wife, but he nevertheless marries a second in response to some transitory desire and without fulfilling the conditions of having more then one wife, he will inevitably be in a difficult situation. He may be unable to provide the mental and material care to his family, which will suffer greatly as a result.

Conditions of permissibility

It is important to ensure that one is able to fulfil the conditions that make marriage to more than one wife permissible. The first condition is the ability to maintain fairness between one's wives. God says: 'If you fear that you will not be able to maintain fairness between them, then marry only one.' (4: 3) This means that a man who fears not to be able to maintain fairness between his wives sticks to one wife. Only a man who is confident that he is able to fulfil this condition may marry more than one.

Another condition is the ability to meet the expenses of one's wives, children and other dependants. This ability is subject to the different conditions and traditions of different societies and communities. 'Abdullāh ibn 'Amr reports that the Prophet (peace be upon him) said: 'It is sufficient of a sin for a man to leave his dependants in a loss.' [Related by Abu Dāwūd]

The third condition is the ability to take care of, and look after one's wives and children. Again, this ability is governed by the traditions of different societies. God says: 'Believers! Guard yourselves and your families against a fire fuelled by people and stones, over which are appointed angels, stern and mighty, who never disobey God in whatever He commands them and always do what they are bidden to do.' (66: 6) God's Messenger (peace be upon him) said: 'Everyone of you is a shepherd and accountable for those under his care... A man is a shepherd of his household and is accountable for his flock.' [Related by al-Bukhari and Muslim]

Reasons for having more than one wife

Several reasons may create a need for having more than one wife. The first is to deal with some family problem. One such problem normally mentioned in this regard is the wife's inability to have children. The desire to have children is a perfectly natural one which Islam also encourages. Maʿqil ibn Yasār mentions that God's Messenger (peace be upon him) said: 'Marry a motherly and friendly woman, as I want to have the largest community.' [Related by al-Nasā'ī] Another problem is that a woman may have some physical defect or a negative characteristic that deprives her husband of feeling happy. On the other hand, a wife may suffer from a chronic physical or mental disease that has a negative effect on family life. It should be noted that in all three cases, a second marriage is a better option than divorcing the first wife.

The second reason is meeting an important need of the man. For example, a man may need to travel frequently and remain absent for extended periods. It may be very difficult for his wife to accompany him on such journeys, because they have young children, or for some other reason. He needs a woman to look after him during such travels.

9. This is one of the reasons normally stated by Fiqh scholars, but this reason seems to better apply to past generations. The ease of modern travel makes it unlikely, except perhaps in rare cases.

A third reason is doing an act of kindness to a good woman who needs a carer. This may be the case of an old woman, or a widow left with young children and who cannot earn their living, or one with some other difficulty. When the case is presented to the first wife, she may be agreeable, or at least she does not express very strong objections.

Such an act of kindness may apply on a wider scale, in communities where women significantly outnumber men. This occasionally occurs in peace time, but more so after wars. The Prophet refers to this phenomenon in two hadiths, speaking of its serious effect in periods of turmoil. Abu Mūsā al-Ashʿarī quotes the Prophet: 'A man is seen to be followed by 40 women, seeking his help, because of the small number of men in comparison to women.' [Related by al-Bukhari and Muslim] Anas said: I heard God's Messenger (peace be upon him) speaking about the signs of the Last Hour. He said: 'Men will be few while women will be numerous, so that 50 women may have one carer.' [Related by al-Bukhari]

Needless to say, polygamy in such conditions is a worthy practice because it is especially helpful for women who cannot otherwise have a husband.

The fourth reason is the desire to have more pleasure when one is healthy and affluent. The social tradition that prevailed in Arabia prior to Islam and after it approved of polygamy, but under Islam a number of controls were put in place to restrict and govern its practice. These include:

- A maximum of four wives. God says: 'You may marry of other women as may be agreeable to you, two or three or four.' (4: 3) Ibn 'Umar narrated that Ghaylān ibn Salamah al-Thaqāfī had ten wives when he embraced Islam. They all followed his lead and embraced Islam. The Prophet told him: 'Retain four and divorce the others.' [Related by Abu Dāwūd]

- Fair treatment of one's wives. This is a condition stated by God in the Qur'an: 'But if you fear that you will not be able to maintain fairness between them, then marry only one.' (4: 3). Abu Hurayrah narrated that the Prophet (peace be upon him) said: 'If a man has two wives and does not maintain fairness between them, he will stand on the Day of Judgement with one half of him dropped.' [Related by al-Tirmidhī]
- Marriage with one's wife's sister or aunt is prohibited. God says: 'and [you are forbidden] to have two sisters as your wives at one and the same time, unless it be a thing of the past.' (4: 23) Abu Hurayrah reports that the Prophet (peace be upon him) said: 'It is not permissible to be married to a woman and her paternal or maternal aunt.' [Related by al-Bukhari and Muslim]

Manners to be observed when having more than one wife

When a man marries another wife, he stays with his new wife for seven nights if she is a virgin or three nights if she is a previously married woman. Anas said: 'It is the Sunnah that when a man marries a virgin and he is already married, he stays with her for seven nights, then he divides his nights equally, but if he marries one who was previously married, he stays with her for three nights then divides his nights equally.' [Related by al-Bukhari and Muslim]

It is recommended that the husband visits his wife during the day when it is not her turn, so as to enquire after her and that she does not miss him for long. 'Ā'ishah reported: 'When God's Messenger (peace be upon him) finished the 'Aṣr Prayer, he visited his wives, and he would be close to them.' [Related by al-Bukhari]

A woman may not make the divorce of the man's first wife a condition of her marriage. Abu Hurayrah said: 'God's Messenger (peace be upon him) prohibited that a woman stipulates a condition requiring the divorce of her sister.' [Related by al-Bukhari]

There should be no request to divorce another wife. Abu Hurayrah narrated that the Prophet (peace be upon him) said: 'It is not permissible for a woman to request the divorce of her sister so as to have it all for herself. She may have only the share granted to her.' [Related by al-Bukhari]

Difficulties resulting from polygamy

Certain difficulties attend marriage to more than one wife. The first of these is that the husband will have to shoulder greater responsibilities. He will have the responsibility to look after two or more homes instead of one, and the upbringing of a larger number of sons and daughters. Yet this responsibility differs from time to time and from one society to another. Needless to say, undertaking this responsibility in a small Bedouin or rural society is greatly different from a complex urban society. It seems that this responsibility was much lighter in the society of the Prophet's Companions and the early Islamic generations.

A husband who has more than one wife has to endure the trouble resulting from the jealousy of his wives, which is natural to women and leads to difficulties. The Prophet (peace be upon him) said: 'God has placed jealousy in women's nature. A woman who contends with it patiently earns the reward of a martyr.' [Related by al-Bazzār] God's Messenger himself had to contend with his wives' jealousy.

Another aspect is that a husband must always be alert to the need to maintain fairness between his wives. He must always be on his guard, lest he becomes guilty of injustice, whether in his treatment of his wives or his children. God says: 'In no way can you maintain equity between your wives, even though you may be keen to do so. Do not, then, be totally partial towards one to the exclusion of the other, leaving her, as it were, in a state of suspense.' (4: 129)

Regulating polygamy

God has permitted polygamy because it serves people's interests. If adverse results occur in a particular time or society, due to ignoring the conditions and manners God has established, or to the change in people's conditions and customs, regulations should be put in place. Such regulations should take people's circumstances into account and promote the observance of the relevant conditions and manners. At the same time, it should serve the objectives of permitting polygamy. Such regulatory steps begin with an effort undertaken by the Muslim community and its leaders to publicize the religious manners and controls applicable to polygamy, so that these become a clear social tradition. This is then followed by enacting the necessary regulations. By nature, the law cannot address all situations and cases. Therefore, it must be enacted when there is clear need for it, and it must be flexible. It should aim to ensure the implementation of manners and controls God has established. Thus, before recording a man's second or third contract of marriage, the judge must look into the husband's financial status and his competence to look after two or more homes. If the first wife applies for divorce on the grounds of the harm this causes her, the judge refers the couple to arbitration, in fulfilment of God's order: 'If you have reason to fear that a breach may occur between a [married] couple, appoint an arbiter from among his people and an arbiter from among her people. If they both want to set things aright, God will bring about their reconciliation.' (4: 35) If the arbiters can bring about such reconciliation, well and good. Otherwise, the judge may grant the application for divorce.